The Ministering Parish

*Methods and Procedures
for Pastoral Organization*

ROBERT R. NEWSOME

PAULIST PRESS
New York/Ramsey

Copyright © 1982
by the Missionary Society
of St. Paul the Apostle
in the State of New York

Library of Congress
Catalog Card Number:
81-85381

ISBN:
0-8091-2435-1

Published by Paulist Press
545 Island Road
Ramsey, N. J. 07446

Printed and bound in the
United States of America

CONTENTS

Chapter 3
PROCLAMATION AND AFFIRMATION OF VISION

Chapter 4
DEVELOPING A PASTORAL PLAN

Chapter 5
THE PREDICTABLE EVOLUTION
OF STRUCTURES

Chapter 6
WHAT HAPPENS TO CENTRALITY PURPOSIVENESS AND PRESENCE?

Chapter 7
THE HEART OF THE MATTER OF STRUCTURAL ALTERNATIVES

Chapter 8
THE CONSTRUCTION AND FUNCTIONING OF A CENTRALITY MODEL

Chapter 9
A PARISH COUNCIL AND
THE CENTRALITY MODEL

Chapter 10
THE FUNCTIONING OF A PARISH
COUNCIL IN A RESEARCH
AND DEVELOPMENT ROLE

ACKNOWLEDGMENTS

In a project of this magnitude, it is impossible to thank everyone who has made a contribution. The writing of a book and all that precedes the decision to grapple with trying to put experiences and thoughts into words is truly a family undertaking. Therefore, I would like to acknowledge especially my dear wife, Charlene, and our sons, Robby and Brendan. A very special thank you and my deepest gratitude to Mrs. Gussie Corradino, my executive assistant, for typing the early drafts of this book and ushering the later drafts through all stages of production with her usual cheerful competence. I owe a special debt of gratitude to Sister Roberta Hackendorf, I. B. V. M., of Ballarat, Victoria, Australia, who came to the Institute for a one-day visit, which lasted three months. During this time, she meticulously worked day and night, helping to finalize the draft submitted for publication.

My greatest debt for the writing of this book is owed to the fifty-seven parishes across seven dioceses, without whom there would be no practical, pastoral experiences worth sharing. Among these parishes, I am particularly grateful to the Pastors of the *Parish Corporate Renewal Network* in the Archdiocese of Chicago, Illinois, and the Pastors of the *Pastoral Alliance for Corporate Renewal* in the Diocese of Toledo, Ohio. I would particularly like to thank those who devoted their time and personal sacrifices to shape, form and finance the Parish Renewal Institute, particularly Bishop Albert Ottenweller, Diocese of Steubenville, Ohio, Bishop John Sullivan, Diocese of Kansas City, Missouri, Monsignor Jack Egan, Notre Dame University, Notre Dame, Indiana, Father Raymond Goedert, St. Barnabas Parish, Archdiocese of Chicago, Illinois, Father Leo Mahon, St. Victor's Parish, Archdiocese of Chicago, Illinois, Father John Blaser, Office of Continuing Education for Priests, Diocese of Toledo, Ohio, and Father Emery Ignacz, St. Mary's Parish, Tiffin, Ohio. I would also like to acknowledge the American Board of Catholic Missions and the Raskob Foundation—the former, for contributing substantial funds for the research preceding this book, and the latter for funding the audio-cassette series which laid the foundation for the writing of this companion book.

A final and most certainly substantial debt of gratitude is owed to numerous Institute staff and consultants whose ideas and hard work have influenced the efforts which made this book possible. Although many other people made significant, intermittent contributions, special acknowledgment is due Fathers Peter Campbell and Larry Gorman, Mr. Patrick Trainor, Dr. Richard Westley and Sister Nancy Westmeyer for their sustained hard work. The final responsibility for the content, of course, is mine.

Preface

The close of the Second Vatican Council in December, 1965 signaled the end of the beginning of a profound struggle within the largest Church of Christendom. The breadth of the Council's vision escapes summary. A call was issued to the Church to transform itself both individually and organizationally and to renew itself in a manner consistent with the patterns with which it would relate to the rest of the world. Fifteen years later the struggle is still more of an experience than something understood.

The world's largest Christian organization—an immense people advancing slowly across the centuries—suddenly declared an intention to move from centering on Christian orthodoxy to forging the leading edge of Christian pilgrimage. So extensive are the possibilities for change that nothing seems capable of standing without question. Catholicism undulates with the turbulent new mood of opened windows, crumbling walls and broken ties. It is a questing, divided Church with colliding purposes and diverse visions. The experience is painful, particularly for those few individuals who feel the wrenching pain of clutching for the reins.

While the Catholic Church as an organization faces constant and formidable challenge to its integrity, Catholics as a people are displaying remarkable tenacity, suggesting the beginning of deeper communion and new vigor. The author views what is occurring and sees emerging foundations for ethnic Catholicism, human ties of heritage and destiny anchored in the common faith rooting deeper than the ties to fatherland. Like the four thousand year old people from which we emerged, our religious and social histories are merging, giving birth to a socially alive Catholicism. This same Church adapting in the past, replenishing and renewing itself through the centuries, is suddenly moving with faith into the unknown with tremendous urgency and deep sense of purpose.

To appreciate this phenomenon, one must understand that the Catholic Church is not a *religion* but a *people* who have walked, are walking, and will walk with a God who will be what he will be. This is confirmed by reading the divine name in Exodus 3:14: "I will be who I will be."

We are, but are not yet, a *people*. We are getting there, of course, but the task of being a *people* requires that we fully grasp and concretize our future. In contrast to the Hellenic view of life in which the future was meaningless, the Hebrews lived in continued expectation.

Faith is not simply "completed in action" but, for its very understanding, faith demands to be "discovered in those actions" of a people, struggling to discover and forge the meaning of their future, their destiny. Our experience of God is born in harmony with the collective forces of social and psychological change which we experience as a people.

Our Lord is God who stands before us, beckons us and calls us. His transcendence is revealed precisely as the force of our future. Jesus speaks of the presence of the kingdom of God but always in terms of God's *coming* kingdom. Futurity and futurism are fundamental to the Jesus message.

Partly because of our own lethargy, and partly because of the richness of the biblical story and the power of the life of Jesus, the Catholic people are always tempted to look backward to those great events when renewal took place, rather than to look toward the future when even greater renewing events lie in store for us. The Catholic people frequently lose sight of Jesus' radical commitment to newness. He established a new covenant, brought a new age, and opened the way to a new future. To be faithful to him, to cease being a *religion*, to become fully his *people*, we need not only a future orientation, but also a methodology to grasp our destiny walking with him who walks before us.

Today Catholics are experiencing increasing conflict, but this conflict is not in the doctrinal or

1

dogmatic arena, as in the past. Rather, the conflict is about the responsibility of the local church to take upon itself the tension between being faithful to our past and faithful to our future. How can we be faithful to our rich inheritance while embracing and shaping our future? Ultimately, the deepest conflict born out of this tension is over change itself. Our greatest (it can almost be said, our *only*) problem is intelligently and faithfully to face, with courage, the change required if we are to keep meeting the Lord before us.

It is the sensitivity to this conflict, the rising to embrace its challenge, the struggles, successes and failures emanating from the efforts of thousands of people that made the authoring of this book (the first of three volumes) possible. This book and its companion series of audio-cassette tapes evolved together. In some sense, each is based on the other, but the book(s) and the tape series have somewhat different audiences and admit differing approaches.

One of the great virtues of a book is that it is possible for the reader to return repeatedly to obscure or difficult concepts and theory much more easily. There is much more freedom for the author in choosing the range and depth of topics for a chapter in a book than for the limited time provided by the recommended duration of an audio-cassette. This book goes more deeply into many theoretical concepts than does the audio-cassette series.

On the other hand, audio-cassettes lend themselves to simpler and more personal explanation of practical issues and methodology. There are topics discussed in the book which are not treated in the cassette series and vice versa. But each segment of the audio-cassette series follows fairly closely the corresponding chapters of this book, and I like to think that the pleasure of each will be enhanced by reference to the other.

Introduction

The prophetic voice of Vatican II urgently summons millions of disciples for modern times. New "apostles" of this second Pentecost are rising from the episcopacy, religious congregations, diocesan clergy and laity. These new "apostles," men and women, lead movements, author theology and design renewal processes.

Kurt Lewin, regarded as the "father of organizational psychology," said, "If you want to understand something, try to change it!" Modern "apostles" understand this well as they experience the difficulty of forming a people and the challenge of refashioning institutions into purposive organizations. Nowhere is the tension between change and stability more evident than in ecclesial organizations such as dioceses and parishes where the major concern is the effort to adapt to change and still survive with organizational integrity.

These "apostles," not blindly faithful to sustaining institutional structures, believe in the principles of authority and the value of organizational integrity. Among them lies a wealth of knowledge and experience. These persons understand the core tensions and basement issues of organizing and forming people in search of their future.

Facing the Challenge

The *Parish Corporate Renewal Network* in Chicago and the *Pastoral Alliance for Corporate Renewal* in Toledo were formed precisely to discover the art and develop the science of forming the Catholic people in our day. Pilot research in both dioceses, involving the parish pastors belonging to these two groups, revealed that the four focal points of discovery and investigation needed for parish renewal were:

Vision: Who are we? Why do we exist? What are we about?

Staff Development: How do we build pastoral leadership, corporate authority and enable growth in the organizational lifestyles of the Catholic people?

Structures: What are the structures that foster a growth in stewardship and enable the parish to engage in corporate Christian action to those beyond ourselves—mission?

Ministry: How shall we call forth, authorize, form and support ministry?

The *Network* of seventeen parishes in Chicago and the *Alliance* of twenty parishes in Toledo were formed to search for the art and science of forming parish, pursuing the four focal points mentioned above. The pastors within each group promised to be accountable to one another during the effort. The pastors in each endeavor agreed to present whatever success or failure, glory or pain that might come in the process as a gift to the Church at large. These thirty-seven parishes comprise 48,341 families, 186,879 people. They are served by core staffs involving 88 full-time laity, 72 religious women and 97 priests. Their effort to plan conscious systemic change within so large a group should be of immense interest and value to the Catholic people.

The Institute of Parish Renewal and Local Church Revitalization

The decision to inaugurate the pilot effort of the *Parish Corporate Renewal Network* was reached on Friday, January 7, 1977 in my living room, only a few feet away from the study where this book is being written. Six months later, the *Pastoral Alliance for Corporate Renewal* inaugurated its pilot effort on Tuesday, June 21, 1977. Concurrently with the development of the Network and Alliance emerged the founding of the *Institute of Parish Renewal and Local Church Revitalization,* an offspring of the *Internal Corporate Renewal Institute.*

In March 1978, the Institute was incorporated as a not-for-profit corporation, organized to provide staff and consultative resources to parishes, alliances of parishes and dioceses engaged in developing and applying the art and science of corporate revitalization and renewal. Institute staff and consultants are an interdisciplinary team of theologians, organizational and applied psychologists, parish administrators and educators, comprised of lay men and women, religious and diocesan clergy who consult or enter into long-term contractual partnerships with others for the purpose of parish and diocesan renewal.

The work of the Institute quickly expanded beyond its service to, and opportunity to learn from the experiences of, the *Network* and the *Alliance*. At the writing of this book, the Institute has been involved in the renewal efforts of eighty-one parishes across eight dioceses. This year the Institute will expand to provide extensive consultation to parishes and alliances of parishes in at least two and possibly three to four additional dioceses. This will also probably be the year that the fruits of its previous efforts are extended to another continent.

Emphasis on Corporate Renewal

The Institute emphasizes organizational rather than only individual or personal renewal. We hold that the word of God is revealed through the experiences, reflection, choices and actions inherent in the collective Christian endeavor. Therefore, we believe that systemic change is more important than solely personal conversion because systemic change, properly accomplished, will encourage and enable individual growth and conversion. Individual change efforts alone often fail or are frustrated unless they are mediated by corporate development that produces planned change in the Church (renewal) and in the world (justice).

Development of Internal Resources

Institute staff do not wish to present themselves as the "total experts" or as the external change agents who provide all the answers and direction. We primarily seek to help develop and work with the internal resources of parishes, networks and dioceses so that they remain the primary resources and authors for the solutions to their own problems and challenges. We call our emphasis *internal corporate renewal* because we believe that the spirit, desire and best resources for renewal are the internal agents for change. It is their experiences, ideas and plans which should be nurtured, educated, brought out, confirmed and polished.

Developing and Resourcing Networks

The task of renewing parishes and dioceses requires resources and cooperative efforts that are well beyond the internal capability of any one parish or diocese. The Institute's essential mission is to develop "networks" through the formation of alliances of parishes and dioceses for a minimum of three years. The purpose of forming these temporary alliances (networks) is to research, develop and apply the art and science of corporate renewal. The Institute provides the vehicle and resources, operating as a catalyst for cooperative efforts across dioceses and among parishes. Our cumulative knowledge and experience enable successive network endeavors to progress more rapidly and delve more deeply into the essential problems of corporate renewal.

Important Implications for All Corporate Endeavors

The last decade has produced volumes of theories and methods for the management of planned change. Processes have been discovered, developed and tested, enabling organizations to change and still maintain their character, integrity and viability as organizations. Generally, these organizations are governmental, educational, health care or some other secular organization rendering a human service or product.

The tasks of renewing and building the Church exhaust the limitations of these sciences when the core values which ultimately give meaning to life are at stake. While theories and methods for organizational development derived from outside the sphere of Christian organizations have contributed to the development and growth of ecclesial collective endeavors, the contribution has virtually never been reciprocal. No systematic attempt has been put forth to gather the experience of these contemporary "apostles" of change, articulating the struggles and tensions inherent in the task of renewing Church.

The challenge of corporate revitalization is not unique to the Catholic people. Within the current struggle to build the Church in the modern world the difficulties are ultimately rooted in factors which are common to all people striving to build corporate foundations. The issues are wider than the Church. The author sincerely believes that these three volumes will prove a significant contribution to the profound need to rediscover a value-based foundation for the relationships among individuals involved in all collective, corporate endeavors.

Chapter One
Putting the Book in Perspective

Many blame the Council of Trent in the sixteenth century for the pre-Vatican II rigidity of the Roman Catholic Church. Such a judgment is both unfair and inaccurate. Many of the issues that we see today as so modern and controversial were being discussed openly in the Catholic Church until the latter part of the nineteenth century. It was the First Vatican Council, under the leadership of Pius IX, which shut down open discussion, imposed authoritarian rule and froze Church structures. This "deep freeze" extending to every area of Church life—dogma, morals, ministry, liturgy, Scripture— was maintained intact until Vatican II when the thaw, so sudden and unprepared for, caused a flood of questions and an avalanche of confusion and defections.

Although the Church in the United States lived through that century-long freeze, it was the phenomenal immigrant flow from Europe that shaped its unique form and vitality. The parish in the United States recreated the villages of Ireland, Poland, Germany, etc., under the parish priest who became the community leader. This type of community and leadership provided identity, protection, education, tradition and hope for millions of poor Catholics who came to a strange land in search of a dream. The immigrants gladly paid the price for these benefits with loyalty and support. Generally, the issues of lack of participation in decision-making, rigid moral and dogmatic pronouncements, paternalism and clericalism were not raised.

However, as the sons and daughters of the immigrants began to go to college, to move up the social scale, to enter the mainstream of American life, the ground under the immigrant Church began to tremble. The movement assumed earthquake proportions when Vatican II released the pent-up emotions, questions, doubts and frustrations of almost a hundred years.

Time of Transition

Now, a generation after the closing of Vatican II, we ask the questions: Is the parish alive or dying? Are Catholics indifferent to the parish? The parish is in a tenuous position but remarkably important to Catholics. With all the painful things that have happened in the last fifteen years in the Church, some delightful things have also occurred. One is the confirming of a basic intuition: "Church" takes place among people, and therefore the bulk of Christian experience occurs in the parish, not in the upper Church structures, or even in the movements. Rather it does, or it doesn't, happen at the parochial level. The parish is where the people are. That's where they experience common-union (communion), the being and becoming the people of God.

In the 1980's what should the parish be and do? Formerly, parishes were marked out and built on two principles: Sunday Mass within walking distance for all the people and a grade school for all Catholic children in the area. Today, in a vastly different Church and world, new parishes must be formed and older ones renewed. How? With what norms? There is needed an art and science of forming the parish. The process of discovering the art and developing that science ought to be of great interest to social scientists who recognize the possibilities of systemic change, to the leaders of the Church because the parish is the very heart of the Church, and to all Christians who are aware of the fact that Christianity cannot be practiced alone, but only as a collective (corporate) people.

The Four Entry Points of Parish Renewal

In the pilot efforts of both the *Parish Corporate Renewal Network* in Chicago and the *Pastoral Alliance For Corporate Renewal* in Toledo, four seemingly separate and distinct entry points for parish renewal were identified, likened initially to the four legs of a chair. It was apparent that substantive parish renewal had to grapple with all four facets: vision, staff development, structures and ministry, and it seemed as if the four facets would have to be embraced simultaneously. As I look back three and a half years, what was being said about each of these entry points?

Vision

In the earliest book of Christian practice (Acts of the Apostles), the proclamation of the "good news" changes several times depending on the teller, the audience and the circumstances. The word of God must be thrilling, intelligible, inspiring, new, or else it is not the "good news." Alone, no compilation of dogmas, no ancient creed, no catechism can contain the Christian message which each community can live by and believe. It must come from the heart of the people, as well as from the soul of the ancient tradition.

The handing down of faith does not mean the imparting of ideas only, but rather the sharing of an experience of God, of Jesus, of grace, of fear and sin, yes, but also the experience of love and hope for the future. This sharing will have to be done by praying together and sharing experiences of God and life in the common fund of stories, current experiences (good and bad) and hopes, dreams and aspirations. All of this indicates a 180 degree turn in pastoral practice and theory.

Staff Development

Not very long ago, the pattern of authority in the Church was only clerical and vertical. Reaction to this pattern has been so negative that those in positions of responsibility in the Church are finding it difficult to achieve significant leadership.

How to achieve leadership without being either authoritarian or passive, how to build a team with sisters and laity, how to "hire and fire," how to establish a commonly held vision, how to pray together, how to discern the Spirit—these are all skills that must be developed. Nothing in their training or former practice prepared priests or sisters for this type of staff relationship.

Structures

There can be little doubt that both functionally and numerically the present structures of parish (hand-me-downs from another kind of Church and age) are inadequate to present and future needs. What must come is a new faith-filled, purposive organization conscious of its need to minister to itself and serve the world to which it is a sign. It would be foolhardy to expect the universal Church to change structures from the top. That would merely reinforce the present process of change which is already inadequate. So the awakening local church (parish) must evaluate its present structures in the light of its new vision and then create new ministries. These new ministries may later be evaluated and perhaps authorized by the universal Church.

The "new" parish then will be a very different model from the pre-Vatican II model. It will look different, act differently and be far more conscious of itself and its roles as sign and servant to the world. Present Church leadership, in general, does not impede the development of such parishes, but neither is it urging them forth. Present Church structures demand little or no accountability to former ideals and practices, nor do they author greater parishes, holding leaders accountable for the kind of parish the people and world need.

Ministry

The priests of today and tomorrow must learn to preside in the center, but not rule over the Catholic people. They must not impose their authority. They must no longer monopolize ministry, but must discern ministries, coordinate them and offer the proper formation, authorization and support for those entering ministry.

The formation of emerging ministries is essential. It is also important that this formation be closely integrated with the experience of the collective vision and purpose of the parish. Therefore, the diocese can no longer be the sole source for selecting, forming, authoring and supporting ministry.

Getting a Grip on the Elephant's Toe

Bishop Albert H. Ottenweller, ordinary of the Diocese of Steubenville, is well known to the Catholic people of America for his passionate speech to the American bishops in 1975 addressing the importance and pressing needs of the parish. He's fond of saying, "You can turn an elephant over by its toe, if you get a good tight grip on that toe." For the pastors, in both the *Alliance* and the *Network*, the problem was which toe to grasp? With which entry-point should they begin? Much discussion finally yielded a three-phase approach:

Phase I: Vision and Staff Development

Phase II: Vision and Engaging Laity in Leadership and Ministry

Phase III: Vision and Reconstruction of Structures for Mission

The issue of vision was pervasive and would be embraced in each of the three phases. Staff development, in concert with vision, would be addressed first, because that's where they were experiencing the greatest confusion, the most pain, and desperate urgency. Every one of these pastors felt confident and competent in his relationship with the Catholic people, in marked contrast to his confusion and uncertainty regarding role and responsibility with staff.

The second phase would sustain emphasis on vision and embrace all facets of engaging the laity in pastoral leadership and ministry. The third phase would address vision and reconstruction of structures for mission. Nearly three years later, it became readily apparent to me that an alliance (or network) of parishes could not reconstruct structures for mission without systematically integrating parish and diocesan renewal through the formation of a pastoral alliance of bishops cooperating to make such an endeavor possible.

What in the beginning looked like a four-legged chair turned out, in a short time, to be a three-legged stool, one leg of which required effective interdependence among at least a few ordinaries and between themselves and a dedicated minority of pastors within each of their respective dioceses. This interdependence, though not easily established, is essential to the corporate renewal of the people of God.

The Scope of This Book—Volume I

The most developed aspect of our consultation is in helping parishes (and networks of parishes) engage the pastoral challenges of developing a parish vision, pastoral plan (strategy) and structure. Specific issues addressed are:

1. *Vision:* How does a parish discern and proclaim a corporate, unifying vision which articulates where the parish *is* and *is called to be*, recalling the faith history of its people?

2. *Strategy:* How does a staff and parish evaluate and develop what it is doing individually and collectively to ensure more effective ministry in light of its parish vision.

3. *Structure:* How can a parish improve its structure for effective communication, accountability and pastoral leadership? How do various groups, e.g., parish council and organizations, relate to this structure?

This book (Volume I) is about the most developed facets of our Phase I consultation. The primary focus of this phase is to face the dual challenge of discerning vision and developing pastoral capability to enable a parish to become a people—a visible sign of the presence of Christ. Our first step is not a course for laity (new ways to change them) but, rather, a mutual grounding in a deep sense of communion out of which life and service together flow. Communion is building together, always in process, never a state sought, caught and statically clung to. To rediscover this sense of communion seems to be the thrust of the Phase I frontier.

Perhaps another way to sketch the focus of this new frontier more concretely is to express it this way. We need to constantly discover new ways for people to be at home. Parishes need to understand that renewal is not simply a one-shot task, but, rather, an on-going process at the very heart of Christian existence, a process by which we must continually seek to rediscover our communion around a common vision and mission, discover our commitment to it, and translate it into organizational form. It is not only an individual process, but a corporate process. It calls for new skills and awareness within the parishes concerning interpersonal relations and how people organize themselves in terms of communion and gospel living. It also calls for the rediscovery of the theology of such a process, or discerning the theological realities within such a process.

As I write this, I am very aware that most parishes (probable ninety-five percent) will begin renewal (revitalization) with conversion experiences and "training" exclusively for the laity. It's easier to change others than it is oneself. This used to bother me, but not anymore. The more parishes help laity to appreciate their rightful role and responsibility in the Church and their right to ministry, the more these parishes will need to know what we learned, beginning where we did. The reverse is also true. There are two ways to skin a rabbit: you can start at the head or the tail. I still believe in beginning at the end of the rabbit we started at, but I'm always glad to help when those who started at the other end find themselves struggling with our end of the rabbit. God knows (and so do they), we will be making full use of their wealth of experience in Volume II.

The Scope of Volume II

Even as Volume I is being printed, the work on writing Volume II has begun. Volume II is about the on-going training, formation, and support of those assuming responsibility for pastoral leadership—to truly lead the ministry of others. Its scope encompasses not only how to prepare laity for pastoral leadership, but also how to prepare other laity, the staff and clergy as well. Volume II shows how different leadership styles reflect various ecclesiologies and theologies and vice versa. It addresses alternatives for calling, forming and supporting the faithful who enter ministry. It also discusses the need for experiences for small group faith-sharing opportunities which provide mutual ministry, support and nurture outreach. It delves deeply into the excitement and challenge of empowering or participating in a parish ministry team. Finally, it addresses experiences for healing, reconciling and calling home the marginal, the alienated and the disenfranchised people of God. This book will also be truly pastoral, weaving theory with the successes and failures from which the book is born.

The Scope of Volume III—Appreciating the Diocesan Challenge

As the American church is discovering a new meaning and relevance of parish, we see the beginning of new momentum and excitement accompanied by the strongly felt sense that something needs to be done for the American diocese.

The pastoral responsibilities and challenges facing an ordinary are overwhelming, and it is no easy task to stay ahead of the problems. It is difficult, if not at times impossible, to move beyond satisfying needs and providing services in order to define the real work of the diocese. It is difficult to discern a contemporary vision for a diocese but even more difficult to develop structures for announcing and proclaiming that corporate vision. Ordinaries face immense staff and organizational difficulties at a time of increasing demands and need for diocesan mission. They face great structural problems.

However, no pre-planned package or outside expertise can provide the answers and direction, nor are the answers likely to come from national bishops' conferences, committees and endeavors. The multitude of meetings that ordinaries are required to attend does not even begin to meet their individual needs for the nourishment and mutual formation necessary to face the pastoral and episcopal challenges of our time.

As bishops, ordinaries are the true apostles of the Church, the successors of the apostles. The need for effective, depth-filled sharing around the great episcopal and pastoral challenges of our time can only be addressed by a small gathering of ordinaries committed to one another and committed to discerning together the real problems, challenges and goals for the "American diocese," particularly as these challenges relate to parish renewal.

The theory of Volume III is completed. At this point I can only hope that when it is published, it too will contain more than theory, but that, of course, depends upon how Volumes I and II are received and the vision and courage of our episcopal leadership.

For Herbie and Phoebe

In writing this book, I have endeavored to be pastoral, that is, to take theory and make it work where people are, blending theory with the fruits of considerable success and failure. The book is written for "Herbie" and "Phoebe," the ordinary pastor, the average associate, the typical staff-person and the average layman. The author appreciates that the greatness of the Catholic Church has never depended on charismatic leaders, but always on "Herbie" and "Phoebe."

Chapter Two
What Is a Parish Vision?

The point of departure for staff development is the same point of departure for planning for the growth and development of the parish. Both must begin by clearly and systematically discerning, articulating, proclaiming and obtaining affirmation on a parish vision. The question is: "How does a parish discern, articulate, proclaim and receive affirmation on a corporate unifying vision which provides the very foundation for "common-union" (communion), "common-unity" (community), unified purpose, direction and action?"

I am not an ecclesiologist, still less a theologian. The focus of this chapter, therefore, will not be to shape a universal, guiding vision for the local church but rather on ways of thinking about the task and challenge of shaping such a vision. To be an effective member of an apostolic organization, one must be able to internalize the collective values and guiding force of a corporate vision. One cannot become a member and belong, much less contribute, to an undifferentiated, disorganized endeavor lacking collective purpose.

The vision which provides this guiding force should not be so exhausted and airy as to be out of touch with daily experience. On the other hand, it should not be so mundane and pragmatic as to contain no inspiration or mandate for growth and change. Our vision of the Church should interpret our collective experience of life, clarifying the priorities and values we hold in common and mandate the ways in which we yearn to be effectively present to one another and to those beyond ourselves.

"Vision" Is a Rubber Word

What is a parish vision? It has been my experience that the word "vision" is a rubber word, meaning that if you stretch it one way it means one thing, stretch it a different way and it means something

else, and stretch it still another way and it means something else. Furthermore, whenever and wherever parishioners, staff or priests gather they can talk about parish vision for virtually days, unaware that they are talking about essentially different processes and methodologies for discerning, articulating, proclaiming and obtaining affirmation on a parish vision. I have found it most helpful to distinguish among three different legitimate pursuits of meaning, value and methodology.

Theologizing

The first of these pursuits involves the discernment, articulation, proclamation and procedure for obtaining affirmation for the "theology of parish" or "fundamentals of faith." It is the pursuit of discerning and articulating simple, exciting and often eclectic responses to the fundamental questions: Who is God, this God of freedom? Who is Jesus? Therefore, who are we? What is the dream of Jesus? What does the humanness of Christ reveal about our own humanity? What is sin, forgiveness, bitterness and healing? What is the Lord's call? What is the ancient challenge of our people, the people from whom we come? What are salvation, redemption, and revelation, and how do they transpire?

The methodology of this kind of discernment does not have to be deductive. In fact, however, the vast majority of Catholic Christians, including the vast majority of ordained Catholic Christians, exempt themselves from this kind of discernment, articulation and proclamation, and therefore, by default, it becomes a deductive process. The methodology of discerning, articulating and proclaiming the theology of parish (the fundamentals of faith) is story-telling and a theological pursuit. Whenever and wherever Catholic Christians gather to discern a vision, there will be among them a very small, yet dedicated minority for whom vision and this kind of theologizing mean the same thing. Most will exempt themselves from pursuing theological vision because they think it's irrelevant and/or they do not experience themselves as competent or confident to participate. Very often the few who uphold the value of this pursuit are accused of "trying to impose their theology." Frequently, this dedicated minority object to this accusation, emphasizing that the right idea of Church has been given to us through revelation, and hence does not need to be constructed.

Reconciling Ecclesiological Changes

The second pursuit for discerning, articulating, proclaiming and obtaining affirmation for a parish vision involves an attempt to integrate and reconcile ecclesiological changes that have affected parish life, particularly in the last two to five decades. Throughout the history of the Church, whenever Catholic people have found their faith particularly meaningful and have lived the Christian life with joy and enthusiasm, it has always been in response to the good news of the gospel *and* a particular ecclesiological vision of the Church. Such an ecclesiological vision of the Church not only gives believable answers to questions like "What is the Church?" and "Why be a Catholic?" but is so moving and so powerful as to generate the kind of energy and enthusiasm that has always characterized Catholics at their best. It is hard to overestimate the importance of ecclesiological vision because what a people takes the good news of the gospel to be is itself a function of their ecclesiology of the Church. Part of the fragmentation of the contemporary *Catholic* Church is due to the fact that there is no agreement among Catholics on that vision. The Catholic community is strung out across at least three different but recognizable ecclesiologies of the Church. In fact, it is not uncommon to find that a middle-aged Catholic has at one time or other in his life held each of the three. Perhaps it would be well for us to reflect on what we have been through as a people *in the last fifty years in this regard:*

The Bark of Peter—the image of the Church in which the Church viewed itself as a great vessel with the successor of Peter at the helm, the clergy as crew, and the laity as the precious cargo. The Church was seen as that institution assuring salvation.

The Mystical Body of Christ—In 1943, Pope Pius XII published *Mystici Corporis* providing the Church with a powerful and dynamic im-

age. No longer were the laity mere cargo, but now were seen as co-redeemers with Christ. The Church as community, emphasizing redemptive fellowship, inspired the Christian Family Movement, Cana, etc.

Conciliar Ecclesiology—Vatican II's image of the Church as the people of God—a purposive "organization," no longer merely institution or community. The local church becomes an apostolic "organization" with a more intense inward thrust (ministry) and a more intense outward thrust (mission).

For many, vision and ecclesiology mean the same thing. However, the vast majority of Catholic Christians feel strung out and internally torn by ecclesiological change. They are angry, very angry, and justifiably so, because no one has satisfactorily explained the meaning and purpose of such changes.

Corporate Challenge

The third and final meaning of what is meant by parish vision is what I call corporate challenge. It is the process of discerning, articulating, proclaiming, and affirming, and, therefore, unity of purpose and direction for a specific parish during a particular moment in time. Methodology for arriving at a corporate challenge is an inductive process based upon the lived experiences of a large segment of the parish. The methodology can and oftentimes does involve everyone in the parish. It is the process that touches on needs, but is more comprehensive than a mere goal generation procedure. The heart of the methodology is to discern, articulate, proclaim and receive affirmation regarding the *gap* between where the parish *is* and where it is *called to be* in the two fundamental areas of parish life—ministry and mission.

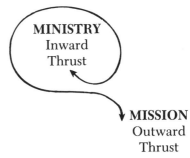

The methodology is expandable and can include as many people as desirable, feasible and appropriate. Sometimes the methodology involves the staff, council and other parish leaders. Oftentimes it

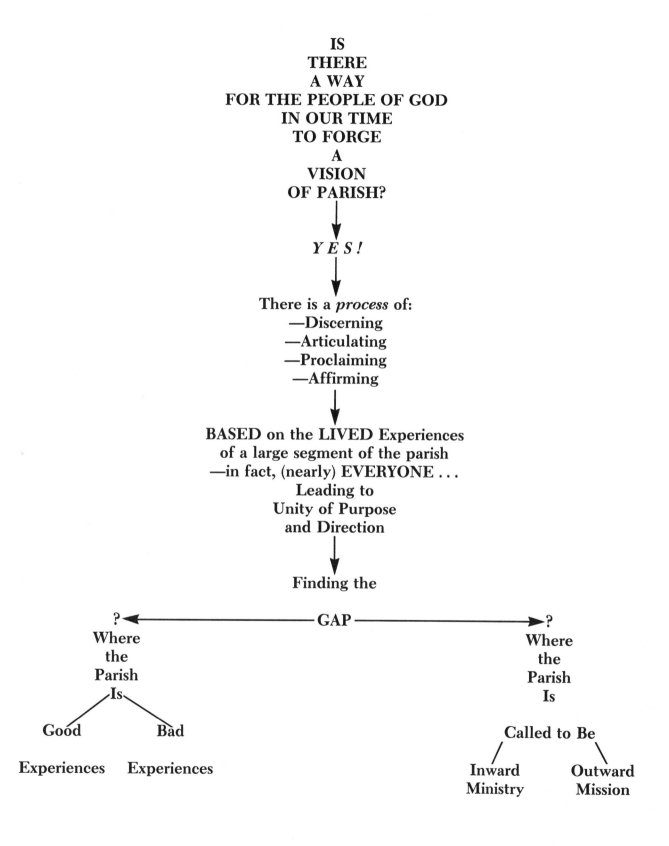

IS
THERE
A WAY
FOR THE PEOPLE OF GOD
IN OUR TIME
TO FORGE
A
VISION
OF PARISH?

↓

YES!

↓

There is a *process* of:
—Discerning
—Articulating
—Proclaiming
—Affirming

↓

BASED on the LIVED Experiences
of a large segment of the parish
—in fact, (nearly) EVERYONE . . .
Leading to
Unity of Purpose
and Direction

↓

Finding the

? ◄─────────── GAP ───────────► ?

Where   Where
the   the
Parish   Parish
Is   Is

Good   Bad   Called to Be

Experiences Experiences   Inward   Outward
                                          Ministry   Mission

involves the staff, council, parish leaders and all parishioners. I'll describe the methodology in its most complete format where it involves staff, council, parish leaders and parishioners, since it's easier to imagine a consolidated, compressed method than it would be to describe a format that involved only a few people, requiring you to imagine a more extensive format.

Attitudes of Discernment

Even when the methodology is going to ultimately involve as many parishioners as are willing to participate, it is best to begin with the pastor and staff alone and apart from the other participants. This initial experience with the staff usually requires anywhere from one day to a day and a half to two full days, depending on the size of the staff. It begins, following some shared prayer and prayerful reflection on Scripture, by asking the staff to go off individually for an hour of reflection, and to prepare to come back and share on the following four questions:

1. What is my most intimate experience of the Lord—that experience in which I most profoundly felt his presence? What happened? How did I experience his presence, etc.?

2. With whom in Scripture or with what scriptural text can I most identify? Why?

3. What is my struggle for conversion at this moment of life, and what is my sin, the way in which I resist that call to conversion?

4. What is the essence of my ministry as best I can articulate it—that which gives meaning to my life, that which I am burning to proclaim and that for which I am most willing to live and die?

My Sharing

I always end the announcement of these four questions with the statement, "These are simple questions," and I always have the experience of their immediate nervous laughter. At this point I very quickly do two things. First, I tell the staff that it has consistently been my experience that it takes about five minutes to get in touch with how to answer these questions and about fifty-five minutes to pray for the courage to share their response. Second, I share my own response to these four questions before they go off to complete their individual reflection in preparation for sharing.

The Precious Discernment Experience

My experience in fifty-seven parishes in seven dioceses has consistently been that this initial sharing to develop the attitude for discernment is a precious experience for the staff. It provides them with the opportunity to understand one another's spiritual journey and struggles. It provides the vehicle to enable them to appreciate where and how they individually and collectively stand before the Lord. The nearest thing to which I can liken this sharing is the experience of a large family gathering late in the evening, following a big holiday meal and cordial drinking, when all of a sudden the older aunts and uncles begin talking about the grandparents or great-grandparents that most of the family are too young to remember. On such an occasion, as is true at this sharing, suddenly all present can appreciate much better who the Lord is, who they are and why they think, believe and feel as they do.

Reflection on Current Experiences

Following the sharing to develop attitudes of discernment, I ask the staff to do some individual reflection on their current experience of the parish (both good experiences and bad experiences) and their hopes, dreams and aspirations for the parish, recording the fruits of their discernment on two pieces of paper—one having to do with the inward ministerial thrust of the parish and the other having to do with the outward thrust or the mission of the parish.

Recording

In recording current experiences, I ask them to record both good experiences (good signs) and bad experiences (bad signs or room for improvement) as well as their hopes, dreams and aspirations in everyday, "pedestrian" language, avoiding clichés, jargon and cryptic phrases. When the staff has completed sharing the fruits of their individual reflection with regard to the parish's ministry and mission, this ends the discernment phase involving staff exclusively. (See examples for recording reflection on mission and ministry.)

Discernment Experience for Parish Leaders

The next step involves the staff inviting the parish council, as well as other parish leaders, heads of the various organizations and leaders of the various ministry teams. During this step, usually forty to sixty parishioners will participate in a format that alternates between time for individual reflection, small group sharing and plenary sessions which tie together the experiences of seven to ten small groups.

EXAMPLE FOR RECORDING PARISH MISSION

What are my CURRENT EXPERIENCES (Good Signs and Room for Improvement) and HOPES, DREAMS AND ASPIRATIONS regarding the quality and scope of our parish mission *beyond* the parish community, i.e., the way the parish ministers to others *outside* the parish?

CURRENT EXPERIENCES
Good Signs (G) and Room for Improvement (R)

1.
2.
3.
4.
5.
6.
7.
8.
9.
10.
11.
12.
etc.

HOPES, DREAMS AND ASPIRATIONS

1.
2.
3.
4.
5.
6.
7.
8.
9.
10.
11.
12.
etc.

_____
Signature

_____
Telephone No.   Group

13

EXAMPLE FOR RECORDING PARISH MINISTRY

What are my CURRENT EXPERIENCES (Good Signs and Room for Improvement) and HOPES, DREAMS AND ASPIRATIONS regarding the quality and scope of ministry *within* the parish?

CURRENT EXPERIENCES
Good Signs (G) and Room for Improvement (R)

1.
2.
3.
4.
5.
6.
7.
8.
9.
10.
11.
12.
etc.

HOPES, DREAMS AND ASPIRATIONS

1.
2.
3.
4.
5.
6.
7.
8.
9.
10.
11.
12.
etc.

_____

Signature

_____

Telephone No.   Group

Thus, the parish leaders complete the entire process that the staff went through, including sharing on the four questions to develop attitudes for discernment and individual reflection, discernment and sharing of current experiences (good signs and bad signs) and hopes, dreams and aspirations regarding parish ministry and mission. Therefore, at the end of this step, there will be forty-five to sixty-eight people who have participated, including the staff and parish leaders.

Total Parish Discernment Process

At this point, an invitation can be extended to everyone in the parish to attend a two evening or day and a half (weekend) "Parish Discernment Process," but not everyone in the parish, of course, will make a commitment to attend. With the staff and parish leaders accepting the responsibility of facilitating small groups of up to eight people each, such an event can accommodate as many as five hundred and fifty participants. Again, following a design that alternates between time for individual reflection, small group sharing and plenary sessions, the participants complete the same process that the staff experienced alone, initially, and that the council and other parish leaders completed prior to this event. Once more, all share on the questions that develop attitudes for discernment and reflect, record and share their own sense of the good experiences, room for improvement and hopes, dreams and aspirations regarding parish ministry and mission. When this step is completed, the discernment is finished, leaving approximately six hundred pages recording good signs and room for improvement and hopes, dreams and aspirations regarding parish ministry and six hundred additional pages addressing good signs, room for improvement and hopes, dreams and aspirations regarding the parish's outward thrust, its mission.

Collating the Fruits of Discernment

The challenge is to now collate all of this information in a manner that will facilitate articulating the corporate challenge of the parish. It has consistently been my experience that a swift reading or review of the material will quickly yield between five to nine broad areas capable of accommodating or assimilating virtually all of the comments recorded as current experiences (good signs or room for improvement) and hopes, dreams and aspirations during the discernment process. The broad areas of challenge will, of course, be unique to each parish,

but some typical and recurring broad areas for sorting the data are as follows:

1. Pastoral Authority
2. Religious and Sacramental Education
3. Liturgy and Worship
4. Marriage and Family Life
5. Stewardship
6. Formation and Discipleship
7. Youth and Young Adults
8. Communication
9. Ministries of Care and Service
10. Evangelization
11. Parish Mission and Apostolic Community
12. Etc.

When the broad areas have been determined that will accommodate and assimilate virtually every comment cited and recorded, the collating begins, allocating every comment listed according to the broad area to which it applies and one of four subcategories within that broad area. (See example for liturgy and worship.)

Quantification of the Fruits of Discernment

In collating the material and transferring the comments to the major areas of challenge which they address, great care is taken to see that absolutely every comment is incorporated into the collated data. Furthermore, during this process of collation, the number of times that a particular item or comment is mentioned as a good sign or room for improvement, etc., is noted. Therefore, when the collation is completed, one has a clear sense of not only what is viewed as a good sign versus room for improvement, etc., but how frequently it was cited, thus adding emphasis as to the extent to which something is viewed as a good sign, or room for improvement, etc. The category "Specific Recommended Strategy" is made a part of this collating process simply because some people can only think more concretely in terms of particular ministries, programs, etc., rather than articulating their hopes, dreams and aspirations in terms of broader ideological areas of challenge. Oftentimes in collating data, the broad areas will consolidate information drawn from experiences regarding ministry with experiences regarding parish mission. Sometimes the same items can be seen both as a good sign and a bad sign (Room for Improvement), thus necessitating that the corporate challenge incorporate the ambiguity or ambivalence surrounding this aspect of the parish's ministry or mission as a part of the collective current experience of the parish.

EXAMPLE FOR LITURGY AND WORSHIP

1. Current Experiences—Good Signs:

2. Current Experiences—Room for Improvement:

3. Hopes, Dreams and Aspirations:

4. Specific Recommended Strategy:

Writing (Articulating) the Corporate Challenge

When all the material is collated, it becomes a relatively simple task to write the corporate challenge, outlining the broad areas in which the parishioners experience a gap between where the parish is and where it is called to be. This should articulate clearly a good narrative sense of the good signs and the room for improvement that comprise the current experiences of the parishioners regarding that area as well as their hopes, dreams and aspirations. The format for writing the corporate challenge in the parish is really quite simple, following the structure of a contemporary Pauline letter. The challenge, in simple "pedestrian" language, usually begins with an explanation of what vision is, in the context of discerning and articulating corporate challenge. It proceeds to put into writing the contemporary challenge which emerges from the gap between where the parish is and where it is called to be, as expressed in the broad areas of challenge.

First Presentation of Corporate Challenge

When the first draft of the corporate challenge is completed, parishes usually find it helpful to invite at least the forty-five to sixty parish leaders who worked to facilitate the parish discernment process for the largest group of participants, and sometimes parishes have invited everyone who participated in the discernment process to gather together for an evening. This evening provides an initial opportunity for those present to review all of the collated material as well as the first draft of the corporate challenge. This affords an opportunity to make suggestions and recommendations for improving the first draft of the corporate challenge, to better capture their current experiences, hopes, dreams and aspirations and to ensure that its writing and language is simple, understandable, straightforward and avoids clichés, jargon and "churchy metaphors."

Second Opportunity for the Total Parish To Shape the Corporate Challenge

Following the first revision, most parishes have elected to mail the second draft of the corporate challenge to every family in the parish, accompanied by a questionnaire inviting parishioners to check whether they very much agree, somewhat agree, do not have the experience to agree or disagree, somewhat disagree or very much disagree with the section on current experiences—good signs, current experiences—room for improvement, and the section on hopes, dreams and aspirations for each of the areas that comprise the corporate chal-

lenge. The following example invites comments in two areas of a corporate challenge—Family and Youth and Young Adults.

Demographic Data

The same questionnaire also asks that respondents provide demographic data regarding their age, sex, marital status, family status, Mass attendance and affiliation to the parish. Other pertinent demographic information is sometimes sought. The following provides an example for organizing demographic data.

Response and Analysis

Our experience has consistently been that between five and fifty percent of the parishioners will read the second draft and provide the evaluative comments requested depending upon how much effort is put into the distribution and collecting of the responses. When this information is collected, it is quite simple to analyze in a way that allows for a simple determination of what parts of the challenge are exciting (or boring) to various groups of people, depending on their age, marital status, family status, etc.

Final Revision of Challenge

Therefore, it becomes possible to systematically articulate a final revision of the corporate challenge with a strong potential of addressing the current experiences, hopes, dreams and aspirations of all the various kinds of parishioners.

With the final revision of the corporate challenge articulated, following the step-by-step inductive process outlined above, the parish is suitably prepared for proclamation and therefore the opportunity to affirm a parish vision that will provide the foundation for "common-union" (communion), "common-unity" (community) and a common sense of direction and purpose.

Example of Parish Corporate Challenge

The following is an example of a parish corporate challenge. In this particular parish, the discerned experiences of all who participated were initially sorted and quantified in eight areas: family, youth and young adults, mission, formation, ministry teams, communication, leadership and liturgy. When the corporate challenge was written, they combined some of the areas and wrote the corporate challenge addressing six areas: family, youth, formation and liturgy, leadership and ministry teams, mission and communication.

VISION STATEMENT

Introduction

"I have called you by name: You are mine." (Isaiah 43:1).

Prior to any personal choice on our part, long before we were able to even articulate the profound and inexhaustible word "God," his love has reached into the core of our being and touched us. This is the experience of the youngest child in our parish as well as ourselves.

Our journey from that moment until now is part of a mosaic of stories that forms us as a parish. We continue to be called to renew, enrich, build upon that experience of God. Together we believe that in Jesus the Word of God continues to speak to us, not only in our most inner being, but also in every aspect of life. This faith invites us to a free response that is both personal and communal. Together we are called to build his kingdom, not in some far off place and time, but here and now.

In the gospel Jesus describes the signs of his kingdom. The hungry are fed, the sick are healed, the sorrowful are comforted, the homeless are given shelter, sinners are forgiven, the stranger is made welcome, those who seek are taught to pray. All this will only continue to happen if we share a common vision of how to give these effective signs to one another and to our society. But the whole vision is never given to one person. Each of us has a part of the truth to share, just as each of us has something to contribute to its living out.

This is a challenging time for us as a parish. We have the opportunity to look at ourselves, with all our good qualities as well as our weaknesses, so that we may, in sharing a vision of our future, also share a commitment to bringing it about.

I. Family

I.A: Current Experiences—Good. We believe that the family is the heart of all Christian formation and development of values. It is the rich soil in which faith grows. Parents as the first teachers of their children are faced with many forces today, as are their children, that make this nurturing of faith extremely difficult. Yet they do not share this concern alone. Their children, through baptism, are at the same time part of the parish family and rightfully claim the care and attention of the whole community.

As a parish we have shown this responsibility to our children. Many adults share in the religious education program as teachers, as aides or in secretarial work. Families are also an integral part of parish gatherings such as the parish picnic, workday, Sunday breakfasts, and special liturgies. Yet there is more that we can do to continue to foster these good experiences.

I.B: Current Experiences—Need for Improvement. Parents need help in parenting and in meeting problems that arise in family life. Single parent families especially should feel that they are supported and encouraged. Families are asking for occasions that will deepen their spiritual life together lest the "rich soil" become dry. They want opportunities both spiritual and social that will bring them together as a family unit in the parish rather than separately. On these occasions family members who do not feel they are part of the faith community should be assured of welcome. Families also feel the need for mutual support in fostering an awareness of moral responsibility to live according to Christian values and in developing a strong sense of commitment to them.

While many parents voice these concerns, some need to be challenged to take the faith development of their children more seriously. We all must see the whole parish as a place where young people and adults experience how to live the Christian life together through prayer, sacraments, liturgy, and service to others according to their ability. These opportunities for service will help everyone to grow in a sense of responsibility.

I.C: Hopes, Dreams and Aspirations. There is a strong desire for support to families with children and for occasions that will unite them. We also recognize that although families with children have special concerns, there are other family structures that are equally important to us. We want to respond to each person's needs so that no one feels alone or unimportant. We also want to call forth from each person his or her own unique gift that is for the good of the community, whether he or she is married, single, parent or non-parent, at whatever stage of life, bearing in mind, however, that each person is fully free to choose his or her own level of involvement in the life of the parish.

II. Youth

II.A: Current Experiences—Good. Although youth are part of the family structure, they are a special concern for us. They are becoming young adults in the parish community and need help in this transition. Caring adults have shared with them through formal religion programs and by being part of Search and Crossroads. Other programs have

FAMILY

A. Current Experiences—Good

☐ very much agree   ☐ somewhat agree   ☐ do not have the experience to agree or disagree   ☐ somewhat disagree   ☐ very much disagree

B. Current Experiences—Challenges

☐ very much agree   ☐ somewhat agree   ☐ do not have the experience to agree or disagree   ☐ somewhat disagree   ☐ very much disagree

C. Hopes, Dreams and Aspirations

☐ very much agree   ☐ somewhat agree   ☐ do not have the experience to agree or disagree   ☐ somewhat disagree   ☐ very much disagree

D. Comments: _____
_____
_____
_____
_____
_____
_____
_____
_____

19

YOUTH AND YOUNG ADULTS

A. Current Experiences—Good

☐ very much agree
☐ somewhat agree
☐ do not have the experience to agree or disagree
☐ somewhat disagree
☐ very much disagree

B. Current Experiences—Challenges

☐ very much agree
☐ somewhat agree
☐ do not have the experience to agree or disagree
☐ somewhat disagree
☐ very much disagree

C. Hopes, Dreams and Aspirations

☐ very much agree
☐ somewhat agree
☐ do not have the experience to agree or disagree
☐ somewhat disagree
☐ very much disagree

D. Comments:_____

been provided that are socially oriented so that the parish becomes a place where young people are welcome and have a place to meet others their own age.

II.B: Current Experiences—Need for Improvement. There is more that could be done to provide opportunities for formal programs of continuing formation specially geared to young people. There is a need now to reach out and involve them more fully in parish life and in the civic community. We must encourage their input and communication concerning parish life and activities. As youth become young adults they must continue to see themselves as a vital part of their parish with opportunities open to them that are in keeping with their age and interests.

II.C: Hopes, Dreams and Aspirations. We must be sensitive to the special needs of young people as they move into adulthood. We have, as a parish, the responsibility to provide opportunities for them to serve one another as well as others in the parish. From us they must learn a love and appreciation for the heritage of their faith. Moreover, the parish should provide help for them in choosing a vocation in life and in learning how to hold Christian values in a world that often lives by different standards. Most of all, youth need to see authentic models of adult lived faith in the parish.

III. Formation—Liturgy

III.A: Current Experiences—Good. We believe that to be formed in our faith, to grow in it, happens in a variety of ways and at every stage of life. This is true of us all—priests, religious, laity. Our relationship with God is always open to new depths of understanding and to new responsibilities. Our life together as a community and our sharing in the Eucharist are both the sign and the cause of this growing relationship. Yet more formal occasions for learning are needed if we are to be fully formed and mature in our faith.

There is a special need to provide children with a basic understanding of the teachings of the Church. To this end the parish has devoted considerable resources to a well-organized program of religious formation (C.C.D.). Special liturgies in which they also take part have been occasions for learning and faith development as well. Youth, too, have been given many positive experiences through special programs, such as Crossroads and Search. Adults have had many opportunities to come together to share their faith and provide support for one an-

other through informal prayer or Bible groups. Other experiences such as Marriage Encounter, Cursillo, and parish retreats have also deeply touched people. The one program that has had most far-reaching effects for adults, however, is Renew. It has for many awakened the desire for spiritual growth and greater involvement in parish life. The desire, generally felt, for a deeper spiritual life and the priority it is given both by leadership and by many in the parish is a strong asset.

III.B: Current Experiences—Need for Improvement. Because of all the good things that have already happened, there is a desire on the part of many to deepen their spiritual life through both formal and informal programs of education, spiritual development and opportunities for faith experiences. There is also a need to provide forums where members of the parish can hear informed discussion of current issues affecting the life of the Church.

In the area of children's formation there is a deep concern that we provide them with the very best program of religious formation in a setting that will foster a good experience of religion for the child. Despite the time, effort, and talents selflessly given by those vitally concerned with the religious education of the children of the parish, many factors, such as the time of day for the classes, the setting in a school situation, and class size, contribute to a negative attitude for some parents and children.

We also recognize that adults and youth must continue to take opportunities to know more about their faith. As ministries develop in the parish and more adults are asked to take part in them, new areas of learning must be explored.

The whole parish needs to find in the liturgy an occasion for well-planned, prayerful celebrations that are the work not only of the celebrant, but also of the people themselves. This participation should include children and youth according to their ability. Small group liturgies that often foster a more personal experience of prayer will also give more time for silent reflection and dialogue that is not always possible in larger groups or at Sunday Masses.

III.C: Hopes, Dreams and Aspirations. In order to answer these expressed needs, we hope to provide more opportunities for personal formation for families and for every age group and special ministry. This can be done through improved programs of education, liturgies, retreats, shared prayer, Bible study, opportunities for spiritual direction, and other religious experiences. But we must not lose sight of the need to strengthen existing programs. In every area we must begin to reach out to those who have not yet been touched. For those already participating in various programs, more should be offered to enhance, strengthen and support the individual's growth.

Another concern has been expressed for those whose service to the parish takes time from their families. We must find ways in which the family life of those in ministry will be enriched by it.

IV. Leadership—Ministry Teams

IV.A: Current Experiences—Good. Jesus Christ who unites us through baptism in his mission to proclaim the kingdom of his Father also calls us to an active responsibility for making that reign of God possible. Leadership in the Church means a participation in Jesus' mission. The public and permanent commitment of the priest that places him in a unique position of responsibility does not diminish the responsibility of the lay person to that mission. One of the strongest positive feelings in our parish discernment was in both these areas. People described the core staff as dedicated and strong, working in harmony among themselves and seeking to create a similar feeling of collaboration in the parish. The response to this call to shared ministry is evident in the involvement of people in many parish activities in a competent and highly motivated spirit of service. Teams of people taking responsibility for particular ministries or areas of service is a sign of growth in the parish.

IV.B: Current Experiences—Room For Improvement. These good signs of strong leadership and involvement in ministries raise some serious concerns. Already the burden of maintaining the many good programs and services we now offer is more than individuals can continue to handle without harm to themselves or to family life in the parish. Services can become so time-consuming for the few that the spiritual foundation that gives them meaning is neglected. We must begin to establish priorities by looking at what we are doing now. We must decide what we want to do in the future and begin to call forth additional leaders and groups of people who will prepare themselves to share the privilege of ministry to which we are all called in baptism.

IV.C: Hopes, Dreams and Aspirations. In order that the good work we do now can benefit our parish in the future, it is necessary to set up some structures that will provide continuity. These structures must, at the same time, have a spiritual foundation that is essential to ministry. Any structure must leave room for the spontaneity and creativity which arises when the spirit touches and moves us.

In a parish of rapid turnover, it is also important to continually encourage new people to ministry. By better organizing our efforts, it will be possible to encourage parishioners, including young adults, to prepare for and to assume leadership roles. It is important to continue to affirm those who take these responsibilities. By learning to minister to one another more effectively, we will use the talents and special skills God has given to us for the benefit of others.

V. Mission

V.A: Current Experiences—Good. Jesus, who came to do the will of his Father, spent time with his followers forming a community of men and women who were important to him. He called them friends. But his final words to them were a command to look beyond themselves, to be concerned not for themselves alone, but for the whole world. This same Jesus who calls us "friend," who forms us as a community with concern for one aother, also directs our attention outward. The mission he gives us to go beyond ourselves does not necessarily mean by our physical presence. It does mean to take issue with the problems that confront our society and seek solutions based on what we have learned from the Lord.

As a parish we already have shown a sense of obligation to others. We have often shared our talents and our financial resources to benefit both those closer to home and those in our diocese who suffer from the lack of opportunity to live a fully human life.

V.B: Current Experiences—Need for Improvement. Yet we must question what we are doing and ask ourselves why we are doing it. How can we develop among ourselves an understanding that there is a love that empowers as well as a love that expresses itself in giving? How can we become a community of faith-filled, loving people who see all of life and its concerns in the light of the gospel, where no human need or concern is alien to us and every person in need feels wanted and loved? How can our words and actions as a community be critical to life and not merely social or ceremonial? How can we balance our rightful inward concern for one another with an outward responsibility for the world? We must act upon this responsibility by giving of our time and talents to the service of others in the community and beyond it.

DEMOGRAPHIC DATA

Demographic information to help us evaluate how the vision statement is exciting or a drag in *relationship* to various age groups, etc.

A. Age—please check one

☐ 12–14   ☐ 15–18   ☐ 19–22   ☐ 23–28   ☐ 29–33   ☐ 34–50   ☐ 50–65   ☐ 65–above

B. Sex—please check one

☐ female   ☐ male

C. Marital status—please check one

☐ single   ☐ married   ☐ separated   ☐ divorced   ☐ widow(er)

D. Weekend Mass most frequently attended—please check one

☐ Sat. 5:00 P.M.   ☐ Sat. 7:30 P.M.   ☐ Sun. 8:00 A.M.   ☐ Sun. 9:00 A.M.   ☐ Sun. 10:00 A.M.   ☐ Sun. 11:15 A.M.   ☐ Sun. 12:30 P.M.   ☐ Sun. 7:30 P.M.

E. Family status—please check one

☐ no children

☐ child or children all middle school or younger

☐ child or children all in high school

☐ children at varied age and school levels; some may be out of the home

☐ child or children in college or college age living at home

☐ child or children grown and out of the home

F. Relationship to parish—please check one

☐ experience myself as committed: did, or do, participate in the Leadership of Ministries Programs, Committees, etc.

☐ experience myself as committed: did, or do, minister but not lead ministry teams, programs, etc.

☐ faithful participant in sacramental life and occasionally like to participate in special events, i.e., retreats, days of recollection, etc.

☐ faithful participant in sacramental life but prefer not to participate in special events, i.e., retreats, days of recollection, etc.

☐ experience myself as marginally affiliated, occasionally participating in the sacraments

☐ experience myself as alienated, disappointed, disenfranchised or apathetic

G. I have decided to sign this questionnaire—please check one

☐ Yes   ☐ No

Signature: _____

23

V.C: Hopes, Dreams and Aspirations. First of all, we must learn to minister among ourselves to those in need, recognizing that they have other gifts to share with us. We must allow for this mutual giving so that people retain their dignity and sense of self-worth. This ministry should not be limited to our parish, but must be extended to others in need. On a larger scale, we need to learn the causes of social injustice within and beyond our parish and begin to address these causes in some concerted and effective way. We have not yet used our influence as a group because we are not well enough informed on the issues. We desire to do all this without losing touch with our deep personal faith and respect for all people.

VI. Communication

VI.A: Current Experiences—Good. One thread that runs through every area in our discussion is that of communication. It is vital among ourselves and beyond the borders of our parish. We do keep the parish informed of events through the weekly bulletin. The annual financial report also gives a good picture of the state of the parish. There is an effort to communicate a sense of welcome and openness in the parish in many ways, especially through occasions of celebration.

VI.B: Current Experiences—Need for Improvement. However, there is much more we could do both internally and outside the parish. Until now formal communication has been limited to the bulletin and to church announcements. Better communication will give a clearer picture of the parish to those who seek to become involved in its activities. Making newcomers feel welcome and a part of the parish is a responsibility which must be assumed by every member of the parish.

There is a need for increased communication with other churches and with civic groups, as well as with the larger community. We also have much to share with neighboring parishes and with the diocese which would give us a better idea of what it means to be Church.

VI.C: Hopes, Dreams and Aspirations. We want to continue what we have begun in personal contact and welcoming people. But we want to develop other concrete ways of communication. A parish newsletter is one way to begin this. It would give an opportunity to go into more detail regarding many programs that interest people. It would also reach people who do not go to church. Another way is to make better use of local newspapers and other media. A directory of parish ministries, organizations, programs and activities will answer the request of many for a more thorough explanation of parish life.

Chapter Three
Proclamation and Affirmation of Vision

A vision isn't a vision until it has been proclaimed and affirmed. In other words, a parish doesn't have a vision until one has been proclaimed, to which people can respond, "That's it! That's where we are and that's where we're called to be. The gap between where we are and where we are called to be is what our ministry, our programs, our collective and individual efforts must address if we are to be true to the Lord in our own time and at our own place."

The most arbitrary thing a pastor and a staff can do, alone or in conjunction with the parish council, is to try to run a local parish without a corporate, unifying vision. The vision doesn't have to be their personal vision, but they are responsible for presiding over and guaranteeing that a methodology is implemented which will yield not only a discerned, articulated, unifying vision, but one which has been proclaimed and affirmed as well—one, of course, which they can sanction and implement.

Preparatory to Proclamation—The Three Meanings of Vision Must Be Remembered

At this point it cannot be emphasized enough that the fundamental need is to understand and appreciate the three different, legitimate meanings for the words "parish vision" mentioned in Chapter 2:

1. "Theology of Parish"—Fundamentals of Faith
2. Ecclesiological Vision
3. Corporate Challenge

After a series of experiments with various formats and designs for proclaiming a parish vision and seeking affirmation, I can say, with the authority that comes from varied successes and failures, that the best proclamation must contain all three ele-

ments of what is meant by parish vision. Proclamation should begin with an excellent proclamation of the theology of parish (fundamentals of faith), addressing the core questions that help and enable people to recall and feel rooted in their faith history and united with the universal Church, its historical truths, and the generations that have preceded us. Secondly, ample time should be provided for proclaiming the meaning of ecclesiological shifts within the last two decades to help people understand, appreciate, reconcile and integrate these changes. Finally, proclamation should address the concrete implications for change by a concerted effort to close the gap between where the parish is and where it is called to be as is articulated in its corporate challenge.

If proclamation addresses only corporate challenge, without any time or sufficient effort to proclaim the theology of parish (fundamentals of faith) and/or reconciling ecclesiological changes, the Catholic community invariably begins to feel uprooted, disloyal and disconnected from the historical truths of its people and the universal Church of which it is a part. Quite simply, people begin to talk and behave as if they expect a Vatican representative to arrive and spank them for discerning the unity of their own experiences, hopes, dreams and aspirations.

On the other hand, proclamation which addresses only theology of parish and the historical and fundamental truths of our faith, even though it may be an exciting and stimulating experience, will leave people with a bewildered sense of "But what does this mean for us?" and "What are we supposed to do now?"

Nor is it sufficient for a particular parish to issue proclamation that touches on the theology of parish and the corporate challenge without the opportunity to understand, appreciate, reconcile and integrate the strain of ecclesiological change over the last few decades. Launching and embracing the concrete implications of change called forth by the gap between *where the parish is* and *where it is called to be* at this point in time requires a preceding balanced synthesis with theology of parish and ecclesiological change.

The Evolving Relationship of the Three Meanings of Vision

At moments in the movement of an event for proclaiming parish vision, I have found repeated evidence for the need to begin with theology of parish, proceeding with the ecclesiological dimension, and finally addressing the concrete implications for change if the parish is to be faithful to the Lord in its time and place (corporate challenge). This does not mean, however, that the development of a parish vision can begin with the theological and/or ecclesiological aspects, initially omitting the concerted effort described in the previous chapter for obtaining corporate challenge. Quite to the contrary, to reverse the order of evolving the interdependence of these three meanings of vision has consistently proved a substantial error.

One could object at this point and declare that the right idea of Church containing all theological truths has been given to us through revelation, and hence does not need to be reconstructed. The essential reality of the Church is indeed a matter of revealed truth, for only through faith and God's word do we understand our experience of the Church as an expression and mediator of God's gift in Jesus Christ. We must continually go back to Scripture and ancient tradition in order to rectify our vision of the Church. But we must appreciate that the Church changes its manner of being and acting from place to place and from age to age. If it is to avoid becoming stagnant, losing enthusiasm and purpose, it must be responsive to the demands of the times, for it has to express and mediate God's grace for different groups of people in accordance with their specific needs, gifts and capabilities. Therefore, to think concretely about the theology of the local church or its ecclesiology we must be intimately in touch with its actual pastoral challenges.

A large part of the crisis of the contemporary Catholic Church, I am convinced, is caused by mistakenly reversing the nature of the evolving relationship between these three essential meanings of vision. People with pastoral responsibility study ecclesiologists, who in turn are reading theologians at a time in our history when ecclesiologists should be studying and appreciating pastoral initiatives, with theologians pursuing theological truths intimately dependent upon pastoral experiences and ecclesiological reflections on these experiences.

The Need for Theological Resources

The Church has frequently spoken about God's relationship to man, calling it "revelation." Our relationship with God is certainly historical, on-going and evolving. I like to think of these three temporal dimensions of revelation as living traditions.

Our local churches are the living expression of this living tradition. Each of us as a Christian participates in this living tradition. As Catholics, we say that our whole lives are a religious experience of God's relationship and revelation to us. The measure to which we are in touch with our personal conversion histories, the conversion history of the people of God, and our unfolding experiences of God among us is the degree to which we are alive in Christ and are participating in living tradition.

For this reason, I encourage parishes discerning their vision to invite the presence of theological and ecclesiological resources to aid them by helping to develop or actually proclaim the theology and ecclesiology that will provide a balanced synthesis with the discerned corporate challenge. Such resources help to provide our fidelity to living tradition not only by enriching this endeavor with historical theological truths, but also by enabling the event itself to be seen for what it actually is—a source of revelation and new theological truths.

At this time of broad and deep renewal in the direction and expression of our fidelity to the gospel in the modern world, there is little wonder that we experience an urgent need to rethink, refine and perhaps even formulate our theology of the local church. Renewal does not mean new labels but new thinking and new living, a change of mind and heart, not simply as individuals, but even more important as a people involved in a collective endeavor. For we transcend the weightlessness of our isolated selves precisely in the measure that we express our collective history and the collective meaning of our individual experiences and actions.

Therefore, while we need historical and scriptural perspective on our lifestyle, we must begin to work on the local level to discover the new patterns of our collective gospel response as they will be reflected in the life of each of us. This communal search in discernment should be not only a means of healing and strengthening our collective life and the most important contribution toward discovering our patterns of service to one another and the world, but also our contribution to the deepening of universal theological truth.

Biblical Basis for a Contemporary Theology of Parish

Some theologians and, indeed, some contemporary Catholic leaders have grave doubts about whether or not Jesus intended to found an organized, collective endeavor. While admitting certain complexities in this question, I would contend that the central difficulty is solved once one recognizes that Jesus deliberately selected, formed, trained, authorized and promised enduring support to the disciples commissioned to share in his ministry. The biblical basis for the contemporary theology of parish, I believe, follows the same emphasis on discipleship underscored by Pope John Paul II in his encyclical *Redemptor hominis* (n. 21). My designation of the Church as an *apostolic organization of disciples* is not common in Catholic theological perspective, but it has biblical basis especially in the Book of Acts, in which terms such as "body of disciples" (6:2) and, more frequently, "the disciples" are recurringly referred to as the Church. An "apostolic organization of disciples" is precisely what Jesus did found.

Once we see the theology of the local church in this light, we are well on our way to successfully addressing two serious obstacles to our collective apostolate. To those who say "Jesus, yes; Church, no," we can say that a disciple is neither a free agent, spontaneously living out an independent Christianity, nor a mere infantilized consumer, passively accepting and appropriating what are viewed as arbitrary pronouncements received from above. The theological themes of discipleship within an apostolic organization escape the negative features of an authoritarian, hierarchical, institutionalism which disenfranchises all but the smallest minority from the experiences of membership and ministry. To be a disciple means to be a trusted participant and investor in the dream of Jesus. Thus, the theological emphasis on discipleship helps to support the purpose, the meaning and the value of organization and authority within the living tradition of the Church. Without falling into exaggerations of institutionalism (dying and ossifying organization), it safeguards the principles of centrality of leadership and historical continuity.

Theology of Discipleship

Life in the Church today is not a static condition but a continual movement. Not only do we advance toward a coming kingdom, but we alternate between being called together and being sent out into the world to assemble that kingdom. The theological image of discipleship, therefore, contains an implicit prescription. When Catholics see themselves as disciples, they enter more eagerly into the collective apostolate of the local church and become less and less inclined to relinquish ministry to a very small group of "professionals." The theme of discipleship within the apostolic organization of the local church represents a more modest but more realistic image for ourselves than the "perfect society," "Body of Christ," "bark of salvation," "community of God," "sacrament of unity," "herald," etc. The disciple and the apostolic organization (local church) of which he or she is a member have neither individually nor collectively arrived. Individually and collectively we are learners, trying to comprehend strange experiences and trying to unravel puzzling problems. To be a disciple is to be on the way to full conversion and to participate in the unfolding of our individual and collective destiny. In the Church today, this is what most of us feel ourselves to be.

The concept of an apostolic organization of disciples means that Catholic Christians are not obligated to relate to Jesus as an historical figure about whom one reads in books. They can take on his mind. They can put Jesus at the center of their collective experiences so that they can judge and discern as he would do. This concept of the local church allows us to be more faithful, obedient and responsive without slavish imitation and without detailed instructions as to what we are to do and think on every occasion. In Jesus and with the support of our universal wisdom, we have, in this theological image, the means whereby, as his disciples, we become more responsible adults.

"Discipleship" suggests a call that is difficult and demanding. It banishes the illusion of "Sunday-morning Christianity" and the solicitations of "cheap grace." To be a Christian according to the New Testament is not simply to believe with one's mind; it is to become a doer of the word, a participant in the formation of the collective destiny of his apostolic organization.

Regarding the principles of "discipleship" and its implicit prescriptions, I am fundamentally in agreement with Avery Dulles, S.J., whose *Imaging the Church for the 1980's* (a background paper for the New York Province Conference, "Apostolic Perspectives for the 1980's," Fordham University, New York, N.Y., June 18–20, 1980) so greatly impressed me and influenced me that I totally revised this chapter relying on his insights. In my mind, the only significant departure in our respective thinking about how to best integrate and channel our similar ecclesial experiences, is that he concludes with the notion of *The Church as Community of Disciples* in contrast to my preference for *The Church as Apostolic Organization of Disciples*. I believe that putting the needed theological emphasis on discipleship, in the context of a community ecclesiology, will only exacerbate the post-conciliar crisis.

The Post-Conciliar Crisis—Ecclesiological Fragmentation

The situation in the Catholic Church as an apostolic organization contains grave causes for concern. Celibate vocations have drastically declined, even if, as some believe, the decline has bottomed out. I personally disagree that the trend has bottomed out. Priests and religious are still leaving their vocation in large numbers. In spite of the high interest in religion, especially among the young, an increasingly high percentage of "under-40 Catholics" no longer regard themselves as members of the Church. As near as I can tell, Catholic participation and affiliation continues to decline at a rate of at least two percent a year. Within the last two years, there has been a marked increase in the number of priests discarding or refusing to accept the responsibility of a pastorate. Many Catholics who enter mixed marriages drift away from Catholicism. The vast majority of Catholics reject the Church's position on contraception and a large number reject official positions on issues such as divorce and, to some extent, abortion. Dogmas such as papal infallibility are widely misunderstood or doubted. The Catholic school system is declining and the Church persists in its inability to use the mass media.

There is, I believe, underneath all these factors a more pervasive and substantial reason for the Church's inability to form a sufficient new leadership to assure an effective apostolate for the coming generations. My own best insight into this problem has to do with the Church's post-conciliar crisis of ecclesiological deterioration, which has left it devoid of a purposive, corporate ecclesiological image. The ineffectiveness of our experience of the local Church, I believe, is closely linked to our inability to form an ecclesiological image of Church into which we can plausibly fit what we think we ought to be doing and being.

Some current images of Church are repugnant; others are so ethereal and lofty that they cannot possibly be grounded in our lived experience. It is imperative that we fashion an appealing and realistic image (ecclesiology) in order to act collectively and confidently in such a way that we can both understand who and what we are and take pride in our collective effort.

The image most emphasized by Vatican II was that of the people of God, a concept rooted in the Old Testament, but applied by the New Testament to the "new Israel." For a little while after the council this image was much in vogue, but, if my impression is correct, the enthusiasm quickly waned. The people who gather in parishes found it too difficult to speak of themselves as God's people. Were we really a people at all? Doesn't this sound too Jewish? Is this a going backward to a declaration that only we can be saved? The metaphor of the Church as the people of God embarrassed us and seemed too triumphal to put ourselves somehow above the rest of humanity (Dulles, *ibid.*, p. 5).

Dulles and I agree that other metaphors such as "sacramental sign," "herald," "servant," etc. are simply too lofty and insufficiently grounded in lived experiences to provide a viable, ecclesial alternative. Vatican II, by subordinating the institutional or hierarchical, ecclesial concept of Church to the others just mentioned, is partly responsible for the post-conciliar crisis. Dulles believes that the council aroused general discontent with the kind of ecclesiology that has been dominant for the previous century, but failed to provide an alternative image that proved truly viable (Dulles, *ibid.*, p. 7). The reason for this failure was, I believe, an inadequately developed *apostolic organizational conceptualization* for the people of God. We simply could not internalize that ecclesiology, faced with the dysfunctional split between two equally inadequate organizational images, the Church as "institution" and the Church as "community."

The Institutional Image

In the minds of most Catholics and non-Catholics alike, the prevailing image of the Catholic Church is that of a highly impersonal institution which can be listened to or disregarded but which does not provide access for organized participation. The Church is understood in terms of dogma, laws and authoritarian, hierarchical pronouncements which impose heavy demands for conformity. To be a good Catholic, to be a "member" of the Catholic Church, according to the popular view, is simply to conform to the beliefs and pronouncements of those few office-holders who constitute the institution. In many respects, it sometimes appears to be an immense institutional machine set over against its own would-be members who, because of its structural nature, have been forced to abandon membership to become consumers, i.e., either complying or not complying with institutional pronouncements. The top officers, even when characterized as "servants" of the institution, appear bound by the rigid party line and are therefore inattentive, unilateral and unresponsive to the movements of the Holy Spirit through the legitimate concerns of the faithful. The hierarchy themselves, according to this perception, are constrained by the very same structure. Following the characteristic patterns of all large institutions, they do what makes for law and order in the Church (institution) rather than empowering and expanding the integration of what is Church in the daily lives of all (those disciples) who seek affiliation, membership and participation (Dulles, *ibid.*, p. 4).

In an earlier day, when people were accustomed to being ruled by alien powers in every sphere of life, the institutionalism of the Church caused little difficulty. People took it for granted that they could have little control over their lives and destiny and that someone would (should) have to tell them what to do and believe. In authoritarian or paternalistic societies, an authoritarian or paternalistic Church feels appropriate. In some respects, in some places, the institutional Church, even today, offers relief from the tyranny of other institutions. But today people take a critical view of all institutions. In today's world it is the "organization" (not the institution) which most effectively mediates the relationship between individuals and their society. The term "institution" is synonymous with failure to be attentive, influenced and responsive to the needs and insights of those it claims to serve. And yet, institutions tend to expect unqualified support, devotion and fidelity with no accountability to their supporters. It seems almost impossible to look upon a closed, bureaucratic system which persists in describing itself as an institution, as a loving mother, Holy Mother Church, bride of Christ, the vine, etc. To large numbers of young people and to many not so young, the institutional image of the Church seems designed to control and exploit rather than to empower and nourish the essentially collective endeavors of all disciples.

The Community Image

Vatican II was aware of the limitations of the institutional model, as is apparent in *Lumen Gentium* which treats the institutional, hierarchical aspects of the Church in its third chapter, preceded by two chapters proposing a variety of non-institutional images. Having already briefly mentioned the other favorite images set forth by Vatican II, I believe that what was heard most clearly and somewhat myopi-

cally from the Second Vatican Council was the quasi-ecclesiology of Church as "community".

The "community" image most frequently used to describe today's local church is in sharp contrast to the "institutional" image. This image, emphasizing collegiality, defines relationships entirely in the context of fraternal bonds, embracing a familial image in which relationships are founded on mutual love, respect and appreciation, negating the need for authority. Within this image, there is an explicit emphasis on shared responsibility which frequently is translated to presume equal responsibility and, therefore, equal authority.

While providing a momentary sense of relief from the "institutional" image, the "community" image, when utilized as a way to organizationally conceptualize the local church, is rapidly becoming viewed as a deceptive, poetic and mythical construct to subdue the laity's disenchantment with an institutionalism that resists corporate revitalization.

Since Vatican II, clergy and religious men and women alike have been continually adapting by internalizing modern structures which enable them to become more effective *apostolic organizations.* Both clergy and religious have renewed their relationships and their structures for accountability, communication and delegation of responsibility, etc., with an equivalent concern for access to authority, organizational participation and corporate effectiveness. Diocesan priests view themselves as *in* the organization and strongly denounce a communitarian view of their affiliation with the Church. It remains an enigma to me that so many diocesan priests and religious men and women advocate a "community" image of the local church for the laity, while they themselves struggle for organizational sophistication, shedding both institutionalism and the anachronism of community structures.

I cite this to make the point that "community" *never was meant to be* a viable social structure that involves *all* Catholic disciples—clergy, religious and laity. While "community" may be a valid way to describe what can occur for a *small group* of people, it is a meaningless, deceptive concept to characterize and conceptualize membership and affiliation within the local church (parish or diocese). Realistically, the community image has been nothing more than a poetic way of trying to convince the Catholic people that somehow they are *in* the Church while being *out* of the institution.

While the "institutional" image remains synonymous with unilateral, arbitrary and authoritarian, suppressive controls, the "community" image emerges as synonymous with the withdrawal of both the access to and support of real leadership. In short, the laity can have either authoritarian leadership or no leadership at all. That's not much of a choice. Neither image promotes or enables the laity to have an access to discipleship through a viable structure which allows their participation in the apostolic organization.

Pervasive Misuse of Dulles' Models of the Church

Dulles' five models of the Church—servant, sacrament, herald, institution and community—have been the most widely read and utilized ecclesiological thought to understand and explain ecclesial changes in the Church in the last decade. Although Dulles himself warned against using these models without a balanced synthesis, too frequently, his advice went unheeded.

The pervasive misuse of these models has not only failed to help reconcile ecclesiological change but has also fed the fires of fragmentation, polarization and discontent. The alternating focus on Church as "institution" versus Church as "community" has exacerbated the notion that the presence and support of authoritative leadership is incompatible with the simultaneous experience of collegiality.

It is for this reason, and this reason only, that I felt compelled to depart from what Avery Dulles describes as "the Church as community of disciples," choosing instead to gore the sacred cow of the concept of "community." Any differences between Dulles and myself may, in my own opinion, be more a matter of semantics than tangible. I am not pursuing an argument with Avery Dulles, whom I certainly highly regard and respect as an ecclesiologist. My purpose for drawing this distinction is solely based on my belief that the "institutional" image and the "community" image are equally useless, sterile and bankrupt. As an organizational psychologist, I am profoundly convinced that nothing short of an organizational image that embraces all the faithful, as disciples, can turn the tide against the present ecclesiological erosion.

Need To Shed "Institution" and "Community" Images Integrating Authority and Collegiality

The "people of God" ecclesiological image of Church, articulated by Vatican II, requires that Catholics face the critical need to shed both the "institutional" and "community" images in order to rediscover the complementarity between authority and collegiality. Such complementarity is presumed to be incompatible within either "institution" or "community," but it is the heart and soul of an apostolic, purposive "organization." An in-depth expla-nation follows in later chapters, contrasting "institution," "community" and "purposive organization."

The image of the Church as the people of God requires that we realize that it is the local church as a *"purposive organization," not an "institution" or "community,"* which most effectively mediates the relationship between individuals (families) and society. *All Catholics, as disciples,* ordained and non-ordained, young and old, male and female, *belong to that organization and it belongs to them.* Within it and through it Catholics must deepen not only their commitment, but also their ability to minister to one another, authoring more growth and helping one another to be more fully human and alive. Through the local church as an *apostolic organization,* the people of God find stability in motion as they renew their commitment and their effort to create a new world in a rapidly changing environment. Thus the Vatican II image called forth a more intense inward thrust (ministry) and outward thrust (mission) requiring a concerted effort of *all* its disciples within the apostolic organization.

A local church (parish or diocese) is an "apostolic organization" which is created for a specific purpose in a particular place and time. It carries out a wide variety of functions in order to accomplish that purpose. These two levels of the local church (parish and diocese) do more than simply carry out functions, however. They also develop relationships with other systems, e.g., other organizations, individuals, families, etc. Therefore, every local church is embedded in a dynamic, shifting environment that requires continuing *discernment* of local vision (Why?—purpose), continuing *discernment* of local pastoral ministry and mission (What?), and continuing *discernment* of local structures (How?).

Proclamation of Ecclesiological Vision

I am not raising the ecclesiological dimension of vision to propose the need for a fourth, still newer ecclesiological vision for the local Catholic church. Actually, I'm very excited by the ecclesiological vision enunciated by Vatican II. Furthermore, I am confident that the Catholic people would share this excitement if they could understand the vision and its reason for being, as well as its prescriptive implications for structural and normative renewal of the relationship between the Catholic people and their leadership.

We should remember that Vatican II occurred in the midst of a powerful ecumenical thrust. We remember the council as an event in which we placed great hope for healing the painful divisions of

ECCLESIOLOGY (DOMINANT IMAGE)	MODEL OF SOCIAL STRUCTURE	PURPOSE	EXPANDING EMPHASIS
BARK OF SALVATION ↓ MYSTICAL BODY ↓ CORPORATE PEOPLE OF GOD	INSTITUTION ↓ COMMUNITY ↓ APOSTOLIC ORGANIZATION	SALVATION ↓ REDEMPTIVE FELLOWSHIP ↓ DISCIPLESHIP	SACRAMENTAL ↓ CATHOLIC ACTION MOVEMENTS—CFM, CANA, YCS, YCW ↓ MINISTRY INWARD → MISSION OUTWARD

schism. When it was over, we found ourselves more confused than enlightened by what it had enunciated to help us understand what it means to be a Catholic. Our identity was diffused rather than sharpened by our gracious attempt to heal and reconcile old hurts. Perhaps this wouldn't have happened if the rest of Christendom present at the council had been searching their souls and renewing themselves with an equivalent intensity.

I am raising the dimension of ecclesiology as a significant facet of the meaning of parish vision because for many Catholics (lay and clergy) vision and ecclesiology mean the same thing. Although it is only one of three dimensions, it is an important one. The vast majority of Catholics feel strung out, internally torn, interpersonally estranged, polarized, and exhausted by change. They cannot articulate their confusion, and they certainly cannot appreciate a reconciling sense of ecclesiological progression.

Part of the fragmentation of contemporary Catholics is due to the fact that very few people have been available to help them understand, appreciate, integrate and reconcile within themselves and with each other the meaning of the ecclesiological changes occurring during the last three generations. Having heard some very good recent efforts to explain these changes, I am convinced that most Catholics are not angry about "the changes" in the Church. The vast majority of the Catholic people are very unsettled and angry, and justifiably so, because so little time has been taken or so little effort

made to articulate the meaning, importance and value of ecclesiological changes. I believe this can be rectified in a way that helps heal existing polarization, confusion and hurt by concentrating on the four dimensions outlined in the diagram.

The diagram provides a means to conceptualize the shifts in purpose, expanding emphasis of local church activity and the enormous and significant changes in the structures for collective action, in the ecclesiological progression from bark of salvation to mystical body to people of God. The Church urgently needs a renewed sense of collective purpose and a new conceptualization of how it organizes itself for gospel living that is worthy of the predominant ecclesiology articulated by Vatican II.

The general anti-institutionalism of the 1960's (which remains pervasive today), in combination with post-conciliar images which did not truly prove viable, resulted in acute polarization. Eager to follow the directives of the council, popular expositors of a "community ecclesiology" tended to oversimplify the council's own statements, giving the impression that the true thrust of Vatican II was toward a Church that would be democratic, participatory and pluralistic. The liberals and progressives, delighted with this hermeneutic, were convinced they had won the day, not reckoning with the fact that they had really been talking essentially to one another.

The majority of bishops, pastors and church-going faithful remained wedded to the pre-conciliar "institutional" ecclesiological image, convinced that it proved the only alternative to ensure organizational integrity. If they read the documents at all, they read different passages, resulting in an acute polarization, with each side accusing the other of contradicting the council. After nearly two decades of struggle and tension between these adversaries, the vast majority of the Catholic people became simply exhausted, bored and uninterested. The net result was ecclesiological bankruptcy. In retrospect, the polarization was silly but, I hope, redemptive. It should have been obvious that both the "institutional" and "community" images were vastly inadequate social structures to organize the people of God for the expanded emphasis of inwardly and outwardly directed discipleship called for by Vatican II. We are and will remain in the state of ecclesiological bankruptcy as long as we feel bound to choose between these two inadequate structures for contemporary gospel living.

Proclamation for Corporate Challenge

While it is possible, and even advisable, sometimes, to utilize the outside resources of laity, religious and/or priest to proclaim the "theology of parish" (fundamentals of faith) and the meaning of ecclesiological change, it is a very unwise decision, indeed, to delegate the responsibility for proclaiming corporate challenge to an "outsider." The Catholic discipleship expects and has the right to expect that this is the responsibility of their own local leadership. No matter how good a job an "outsider" might do proclaiming the corporate challenge of a particular parish, he or she just cannot do it well enough to prevent the people of the parish from believing and feeling that their leadership has betrayed them by abdicating a responsibility essentially and fundamentally theirs.

It is impossible to present here content pertaining to the proclamation of a parish's corporate challenge since that will be unique to every parish and may vary substantially at different moments and times. The task of proclaiming the corporate challenge requires the meaning, blending, dovetailing, meshing, transforming and distilling into one story the personal faith-history of the proclaimer and the corporate challenge of the parish. It is a hard but not complicated task. The proclaimer must struggle to merge the collective experiences, thoughts, struggles and choices-for-action with his or her own experiences, reflections, struggles and options.

The proclaimer must struggle to become transparent, revealing his or her most tender inner self wedded to the opportunity for greatness rising out of the corporate challenge to embrace collectively the Lord's dream. At the same time, the proclaimer must struggle to make it possible for people to see beyond him or her—and view the Lord.

I have already said that this kind of proclamation is difficult but not complicated. Adequate preparation for proclamation pertaining to the corporate challenge can easily require thirty to one hundred hours of reflection and practice.

Seminary and, particularly, homiletic training does not give one an edge to proclaim with confidence and competence. In fact, priests usually have to fight to overcome the results of this training. In proclamation it is a deadly mistake to theologize in the academic tradition. Good proclamation is choked by the temptation to avoid one's own struggle and story, focusing all concern on the experiences, tensions, struggles and choices of others. Seminary and homiletic training predispose priests to both of these errors, but the best safeguard is to rehearse proclamation pertaining to corporate challenge at least twice before a small audience (usually parish staff) that is committed to critique candidly and help the proclaimer.

The written corporate challenge provides the parameters for its own proclamation. A brief discussion among staff is usually all that is necessary to decide how to divide or combine the important major themes of the corporate challenge. The order of proclamation is decided, as well as who should take which parts. Generally, but not always, if others besides the pastor participate, it is best to save the pastor's proclamation until last.

Designs for Proclamation of Vision

There are numerous alternative designs for proclaiming parish vision. Some designs emphasize the basic format of days of recollection, each day usually spaced a week apart. Some designs place their emphasis on home and neighborhood gatherings. One parish obtained considerable cable television time, bringing the proclamation of their parish vision, through the television set, to the living room of everyone in a rural community. Although most designs integrate the major proclamation event(s) with special homilies before, during and after the proclamation of the vision, the Sunday homily by itself simply does not provide enough time to carry the weight of proclaiming the vision.

Most parish staffs require five days to design and adequately prepare for the proclamation of the parish vision, appreciating the necessity to do a good job with all three facets of proclaiming parish vision. More time is required, of course, when the staff chooses to prepare to proclaim the fundamentals of faith and the meaning of ecclesiological changes rather than inviting visiting resources to assist in one or both of these aspects.

In my opinion, the best overall design alternative is a parish mission, a revival experience in the minds of many Catholics. Many middle-aged and most older Catholics recognize and associate a parish mission with the notions of conversion and reform—the annual event when we discover again why and who we are and what it's all about. Although initially amazed, I have grown quite accustomed to seeing 800 to 1,500 people (in parishes of 1,000 to 2,800 families) register for a parish mission scheduled for four or five consecutive days. Regardless of the basic design selected for the proclamation of vision, the following aspects should be given careful consideration:

1. *Timing.* The best time for implementing the proclamation event is Lent. However, other times of the year are similarly well suited, but not the summer months and days too close to major holidays. Care should be taken not to schedule this event in conflict with demanding events outside the parish, such as graduations, public holidays, major sporting events, etc. Absolutely all other parish-related activities immediately preceding and during this event should be cancelled.

In setting the dates for the event, it is wise not to allow too much time to elapse between the discernment process and the proclamation event. It is important that people understand and appreciate the relationship between the discernment process in which they participated and the proclamation event.

2. *Time Allocation.* Regardless of the format and design chosen, the amount of time for proclamation is limited. Generally speaking, the most effective formats allocate between fifty and sixty-five percent of the time available for the rooting experience of proclaiming theology of the parish (fundamentals of faith). About twenty to thirty percent of the time should be allocated for the reconciling experience of proclaiming the meaning of ecclesiological changes. Only about twenty percent of the available time is needed for proclamation directly pertaining to the corporate challenge. The concrete implications for change, which it calls forth, close the gap between *where the parish is and where it is called to be.* It is a mistake to divide the available time in thirds and an even greater error to rush through the rooting and/or reconciling experiences

to make more time available for proclamation directly pertaining to the corporate challenge.

3. *Written Articulation of the Corporate Challenge.* At some point in the proclamation event everyone should receive a written copy of the corporate challenge. Most parishes have the corporate challenge printed in a booklet. This can also include a letter from the pastor explaining how it was discerned and giving a short history of the parish. If a printed booklet containing the corporate challenge is to be distributed during the proclamation event, people should be given time to read it in its entirety and reflect silently on its meaning. Don't read it to them and don't distribute it prior to the proclamation event but somewhere during the third and final moment thereof.

In printing the corporate challenge, it is important not to delete the current experiences, describing the good signs and bad signs of each section of the corporate challenge for which there are hopes, dreams and aspirations. It is tempting and natural to want to delete this part of the contemporary epistle, but people need to know clearly what they are leaving behind, what they are walking away from, as well as what they are walking toward. One has to leave someplace to go somewhere new.

4. *Liturgy and Paraliturgy.* Song, symbol, Scripture reading, prayer and the Eucharist may form part of the proclamation event. However, the heart of the proclamation event is proclamation, the emphasis being on the word of God. I have seen proclamation events dulled and deflated because more time, effort and energy was devoted to paraliturgical and symbolic actions than to preparing great proclamation.

5. *Pre-Event and Post-Event "Catechesis".* The proclamation event should definitely be announced and anticipated. Actually parishes have a lot of fun spreading the word and rousing enthusiasm and excitement for the upcoming event. Everyone in the parish should know well in advance. This is important. In many places, every family receives a letter and the bulletin announces the events several weeks in advance. Staff and parishioners extend by phone, in person, or by handwritten letter a personal invitation: "Please come. This is important."

"Pre-event catechesis" heightens anticipation, emphasizes the importance of the event and prepares people for what is to follow. Homilies prior to the proclamation event provide an excellent opportunity for "preparatory catechesis." However, it really isn't "catechesis," since one cannot "catechize" without the vision. The parameters and foundation for catechesis are established by the vision, so, technically, catechesis cannot be offered before the vision is proclaimed and affirmed. After the event, there is not only ample opportunity but tremendous value in providing continuing catechesis on the themes and issues comprising the corporate challenge.

6. *Time Blocks.* If a parish chooses to utilize the format of the parish mission for the proclamation event, it will, no doubt, be helpful to know the time blocks which have proved most successful. I think the best parish mission begins with a big block of time (four to six hours) starting on a Sunday, about 2 P.M. Following this format, the mission continues providing two alternative tracts. The morning tract begins with a two to two and a half hour block of time immediately following an optional Mass, scheduled between 8:15 and 8:30 A.M. The evening tract also begins with a two to two and a half hour block, immediately beginning after an optional Mass scheduled about 7:30 P.M. The morning and evening tracts are identical, providing two options during the day to participate in the same experience. Utilizing this format on Monday and Tuesday, the mission could close on a Wednesday or Thursday.

Another alternative is to omit a large block of time on Sunday afternoon, beginning the mission of everyone on Sunday evening, followed by the same two-tract alternatives outlined above. Many parishes have graciously arranged baby-sitting services and activities at the parish, making it much easier, and, of course, less expensive to participate on all days. This also makes it possible for the parish mission to be a family event by not forcing mom and dad to attend on alternate nights.

7. *Small Group Discussion.* Many parishes want small group discussion to be a component of their proclamation event. This is an excellent idea, but it should not be made a condition for participating. If small group discussions form one option, other equally acceptable options should be presented. While small group discussion proceeds, some may prefer silent meditation in the church with exposition (pre-recorded music may be used). A third option is to make coffee and other refreshments available where people can meet and greet each other informally but not disturb those in small group discussion or silent meditation. The point is that if you are going to have small group discussion, make

other options available and present them as equally valuable.

8. *Small Group Facilitators.* If the option for small group discussion is provided in designing the proclamation event, these discussion groups should be adequately facilitated. The following is a list of suggestions for small group facilitators:

(a) *Opening Prayer.* A short prayer should be offered by the facilitator, asking for God's presence within the group and for an openness to experience the Lord in one another. (1 minute)

(b) *Introductions.* In the first session people should be asked to give their names and just a little bit of information about themselves. If someone new joins the group in a subsequent session, the introductions should be repeated for his/her benefit, but keep the total time for this very short. (3 to 5 minutes)

(c) *Discussion.* The question(s) to be discussed should be announced by someone just before people move into the small groups. The discussion should be a relaxed and friendly exchange of ideas and feelings among the participants.

- Avoid arguments. Ensure that each person's ideas and feelings are respected and reverenced.
- Thank each person for his/her contribution. Reassure all, if necessary, that their contributions are valuable and part of reality and truth and that in no way should they feel guilty or uninformed or dumb about what they have said.
- As facilitator, ask questions and, if asked, answer questions, but avoid teaching or dominating the group discussion.
- Seek the opinions and feelings from participants who appear shy and reluctant to assert themselves, but don't push them to share.
- If you think someone's contribution isn't understood or is misunderstood, try to get clarification by asking for examples, etc.
- Toward the end of the discussion, after everyone has had the opportunity to share his or her own experience, encourage friendly, warm, response to one another. Again praising and thanking all for their ideas and feelings, set a climate of acceptance for all experiences.
- Manage "air time." Try to give people equal time.

(d) *Other Key Points For Facilitators.*

- Try not to give the impression that you are "outside" the group.
- Your own reflections and sharing are important. Sometimes it is helpful if you share first; this will encourage others to share.
- Avoid the "jargon" that others will be unfamiliar with if they did not participate in the discernment process prior to the proclamation event.
- Believe in the goodness of the people in your group and that the Holy Spirit is working among the participants. *Don't become anxious.* The Lord will do the work.
- Gently draw the group back to the topic of discussion if they stray too far. If the discussion is fruitful, then don't rush them. You needn't cover every question.
- Encourage the expression of feelings and not just ideas. Feelings are good indicators of values.
- If someone talks too much and tends to dominate, draw the focus back to the group and encourage the thoughts of others. If any individuals persist in dominating, then speak to them afterward, encouraging them to give more timid persons a chance to open up.
- Don't feel that you must rush in every time there is a silent moment. Allow people to relax and to become comfortable with one another and comfortable with the moments of silence in one another's presence.
- Start and end the session on a timely basis (within three to five minutes of the appointed time). Avoid being so punctual that anyone arriving a few minutes late is made to feel uncomfortable.
- Conflict and differences of opinion are not necessarily bad. They often expand the discussion, but should not be allowed to get out of hand.

(e) *Prayer and Witness.* Allow for personal witness if someone wants to share an example out of his or her own life related to the question under discussion. It may happen in the course of subsequent discussion sessions that you will sense an opportunity to end discussion with an experience of shared prayer. However, be careful not to rush this, since some people are very uncomfortable with such experiences.

9. *Communal Reconciliation Service.* Consistently proven of immense value is the inclusion of a communal reconciliation service as part of the proclamation event. It should be scheduled somewhat early but not at the very beginning, particularly if utilizing a parish mission format. People expect the opportunity for reconcilication, but while one can't start off with it directly, it is nice to get to it, and through it, as soon as possible, providing a better climate for a contemporary parish mission. Traditional missions are renowned for going on and on with an examination of conscience, ending with reconciliation and a pledge not to drink and/or beat your spouse!

10. *Other Considerations.* The proclamation event is a serious event but by no means should it be somber and uninspiring. It's not a funeral, nor is it a time for the hell-fire and brimstone characteristic of the traditional parish mission. It should be exciting, exhilarating and quite festive. Therefore, it helps to begin the proclamation event with a procession of trumpets, song, cymbals and running children. Different sessions or days can begin and certainly end with joyous, happily nostalgic and triumphal song. Evening sessions often end with an invitation to wine and cheese, while the closing event could be followed by a gala parish-fest with drinks and hors d'oeuvres!

Final Comment

It may seem more than a bit strange to title a chapter "Proclamation and Affirmation of Vision" when it exclusively addresses proclamation. Actually, there is little or nothing at all that can be said about the methodology of affirmation. Affirmation is a response.

If care is taken to do a good job and if care is taken to prepare faithfully the discernment for vision process, it will bear fruit.

Since this vision is for its own time only, eager for its own fulfillment, it does not deceive; if it comes slowly, wait, for come it will, without fail (Habakkuk 2:3).

Similarly, it is of the utmost importance to enunciate carefully, clearly and practically and to articulate the vision:

And the Lord said to me: Write the vision; make it plain upon tablets, so he may run who reads it (Habakkuk 2:2).

Nehemiah is clear about proclamation and the affirming fruits of proclamation:

On the square before the Water-Gate, in the presence of the men and women, and children old enough to understand, he read from the book from early morning until noon; all the people listened attentively to the Book of the Law [not the Ten Commandments but the story of who they are and their vision—the Pentateuch]. . . . And Ezra, priest and scribe (and the Levites who were instructing the people) said to all the people, "This day is sacred to Yahweh your God. Do not be mournful, do not weep!"

For the people were all in tears as they listened to the words of the law.

He then said, "Go, eat the fat, drink the sweet wine, and send a portion to the man who has nothing prepared ready. For this day is sacred to our Lord. Do not be sad; the joy of Yahweh is your stronghold." And the Levites calmed all the people, saying, "Be at ease; this is a sacred day. Do not be sad." And all the people went off to eat and drink and give shares away and begin to enjoy themselves since they had understood the meaning of what had been proclaimed to them. . . . And there was great merry-making (Nehemiah 8:3, 8–12, 17).

Chapter Four
Developing a Pastoral Plan

After a parish has discerned, articulated, proclaimed and received affirmation for its corporate unifying vision (which provides the foundation for "common-union," "common-unity," unified purpose, direction and action), how does it make the dream walk? With a good, clear sense of why the parish exists, what is it to continue doing, stop doing or begin to do if it is to be true to its vision and close the gap between where the parish is and where it is called to be? How do a staff and parish evaluate and develop what is being done, individually and collectively, to ensure more effective ministry in light of its parish vision?

In embracing the challenge to evaluate and change ministries, programs and ministry teams, etc., a parish *cannot* separate the task of changing the parish pastoral plan (corporate strategy) from the task of changing individual staff roles. Changing the pastoral plan involves changing what individual staff are doing and how they do it. Any talk of changing the pastoral plan without an appreciation of and commitment to changing individual staff roles is a waste of time.

Current Allocation of Time

The challenge of developing the pastoral plan in light of the parish vision begins by assessing the current allocation of how the staff spends its time. I find it helpful to distinguish four major areas of the parish pastoral plan: (1) individual ministry, (2) programs, (3) ministry teams, and (4) organizations, commissions, councils and boards. Utilizing these four major areas, the staff can create a simple matrix, listing all the areas of individual ministries under that major category, all the separate programs under that major category, all the respective ministry teams that fall under that classification and all the different organizations, committees, commis-

sions, etc. Then each member of the staff, with help from the others, determines as accurately as possible the average number of hours per week he or she devotes to each area of individual ministry, to each program, to each ministry team and to each of the organizations, various boards, etc.

Individual Ministries

Individual ministries include all those activities that staff do alone, as part of their ministerial responsibility, such as weekday Masses, weekend Masses, preparation of homilies, hospital visitation, tribunal work, wakes, funerals, weddings, anointings, Communion calls, individual counseling, etc. In most parishes, large or small, there are fifty to seventy-five different kinds of individual ministries.

The bulk of individual ministries is usually carried by priest staff, typically about one half of each priest's time being allocated to the various activities that comprise this major area. Rarely does the percentage of time for non-ordained staff exceed ten percent.

Programs

Programs include those components of the pastoral plan inevitably run by the staff. Programs are often heavily subsidized and require either "professional" or "trained semi-professional" ministers. Examples are the religious education program, the catechumenate, parish retreats, the school, marriage preparation, etc. Most parishes, large or small, have anywhere between ten and thirty different programs as part of their pastoral plan.

Parishes vary considerably in the percentage of staff time earmarked for various programs. Allocation of staff time to programs ranges from high percentages in program orientated parishes to a minimum of ten percent in others. Parishes allotting

DEVELOPING THE PASTORAL PLAN

INDIVIDUAL MINISTRY	CURRENT					NEW				
	John	Bob	Jan	Tim	Vi	John	Bob	Jan	Tim	Vi
Weekday Masses										
Weekend Masses										
Preparation of Homily										
Hospital Visitation										
Etc.										
Sub-Total										
PROGRAMS										
Religious Education										
Catechumenate										
Parish Retreats										
Etc.										
Sub-Total										
MINISTRY TEAMS										
Ministering to Alienated and Marginal										
Family Search										
Marriage Enrichment										
Etc.										
Sub-Total										
ORGANIZATIONS, BOARDS COMMITTEES, COMMISSIONS, COUNCILS, Etc.										
Finance Committee										
Maintenance Committee										
Rosary Society										
Men's Club										
Building Commission										
Etc.										
Sub-Total										
TOTAL										

Corporate Strategy Development/Individual Role Clarification a substantial amount of staff time to programs invariably have few or no remaining resources with which to author, support and sustain ministry teams. Sometimes a program or programs are vehicles for extending lateral ministry, in which case at least a portion of the time allocated to programs is intimately related to that allocated to ministry teams.

Ministry Teams

The third area of the parish strategy includes the ministry teams. These differ from programs in that they usually comprise a group of laity who minister to one another and collectively address a particular need for ministry within the parish. Usually the laity who constitute these ministry teams are not "professional" or "semi-professional" and so often require much less formal training and do not expect remuneration. Ministry teams include such things as ministering to the alienated and marginal, family search, marriage enrichment, welcoming ministry, ministry to the divorced and separated, etc.

Ministry teams are the vehicle for lateral ministry. The amount and percentage of staff-time allocated to the components comprising this major category provides the best index of the extent to which a parish actually has activated a post-conciliar ecclesiology.

Organizations

Organizations, boards, committees, commissions and councils include the various groups within the parish organized for social functions, fund raising, and intermittent service projects or to assist in functions related to coordinating, planning and governance. This area includes groups like the finance and maintenance committees, rosary society, men's club, parish council, school board, etc.

It is the very rare parish indeed in which more than five percent of the staff's total time is assigned to working with such groups. While the actual percentage of time is always quite small, the emotional drain emanating from the need to be present or to participate in these activities is quite high. Staffs are always surprised to discover the actual low percentage of time deployed in these activities. The emotional turmoil, ambivalence and tensions are proportionally very much greater than the percentage of actual time devoted to these aspects of the total parish plan.

Evaluation of the Pastoral Plan

When the assessment of the current allocation of staff time is completed, not only does it provide an accurate picture of what each staff person is doing and how he or she is spending his or her time, but also a good composite picture emerges of what the staff is doing collectively. It shows what percentage of resources is devoted to individual ministry versus programs versus ministry teams versus organizations, boards, committees, etc. This composite presents a good picture of which components of the four major areas are receiving the largest allocation of staff time.

When the current picture of the pastoral plan is completed, the staff undertakes a stringent evaluation of the parish's pastoral plan, in light of the parish vision, by addressing *three* questions:

1. What are we doing that *is* helping to close the gap between where we are and where we are called to be?
2. What are we doing that *is not* helping to close the gap between where we are and where we are called to be?
3. What *should* we be doing that we *are not presently* doing to close the gap between where we are and where we are called to be?

The third question, of course, requires that the staff determine new components of the pastoral plan, that is, new areas of individual ministry, new programs, new ministry teams or new organizations called forth by the challenge of the parish vision. Furthermore, in creating these new components, the staff must accurately estimate the amount of staff time required to initiate, author and implement these new components.

Two Tensions

In addressing the above three questions, the staff engages two essential and difficult tensions when evaluating and changing what it is doing, individually and collectively, to ensure more effective ministry in light of the parish vision. The first tension arises from the need to allocate adequate and sufficient time to the new components of the pastoral plan while at the same time feeling reluctant, unable or expected to maintain the existing commitments, ties, responsibilities, etc.

The second tension, which is even greater, surrounds the necessity of addressing how much or what percentage of time to allocate to individual ministries versus programs versus ministry teams versus the category comprising the multitude of organizations, boards, committees, etc. This second tension is greater because ultimately the decisions reached with regard to how much staff time is sufficient to allocate to each of these four major areas will reflect the real and actual ecclesiology of the parish plan, sometimes reflecting a marked contrast to the theoretically espoused ecclesiology.

Generally speaking, the percentage of time apportioned to ministry teams forms an accurate indicator of the extent to which the parish has activated the post-conciliar ecclesiology of purposive organization. Parishes allocating a comparatively high percentage of time to a wide range of programs having nothing to do with expanding lateral ministry are predominantly oriented to a mystical body ecclesiology. Those giving a very high percentage of time to individual ministries are implementing a bark of salvation ecclesiology, regardless of what they claim is their image of the Church. This is particularly evident in parishes where the staff members feel a compulsion for extensive presence in the activities of organizations, the primary thrust of which is socializing or fund-raising.

Typically, when staff begin evaluating their pastoral plan, they discover that more than half of their time is apportioned for individual ministry, about a third is apportioned for programs, a small amount for ministry teams and the remainder is allocated for organizations.

Revising the pastoral plan usually means attenuating the allocation of time for individual ministry, reducing the time apportioned for programs, unrelated to authoring and supporting ministry teams, and minimizing extensive presence at social and fund-raising functions. These reductions in time allocations provide more time for authoring and supporting ministry teams and the inauguration of programs related to this activity. Thus, the staff begins more and more to minister to ministers. As parishioners claim their right and responsibility to minister, "the purposive organization" envisaged by Vatican II emerges.

Only the Good Die Young!

While there are, no doubt, staffs who do the absolute minimum (but in my work, I never see them), my consistent experience has been that most staffs are vastly overextended in terms of their current commitments, even before they begin to create new ministry teams, etc., called for by the parish vision. Indeed, it is not uncommon to find that the pastor, priests and other members who comprise the parish staff have committed themselves to so many different things that their current average work week entails eighty or ninety or more hours of *scheduled* time.

These staffs readily admit that their ministry

has, in reality, become extremely reactive, determined on a daily basis mostly by who first gets hold of them by phone in the course of a day. Planning and allocation of time fall by the way. Commitment which in total demands more than forty-five hours per week is irresponsible. It is also a prayer for a coronary.

Overextended schedules and overextended commitments have been the direct result of past changes in the pastoral plan which have been exclusively additive. If someone had what looked like a good idea, it was added without any adequate regard to the individual and collective limitations of the staff. One associate once told me he was sure that one day someone in their parish would approach the staff to announce, "There is a parish a few miles from here that has a special ministry to leprechauns. What the hell are you guys doing for leprechauns here?"

Burning Out Staff, Burnt-Out Laity

Parish staffs, overextending themselves by constantly adding new components to the pastoral plan and not reverencing their limitations, are burning themselves out. It is characteristic of these staffs that they begin to attach themselves to a dedicated and generous minority of parishioners who find themselves repeatedly called upon, by everyone on the staff, to contribute to every activity. These laity soon begin to pray for a job transfer or some other acceptable excuse to relocate their residence far enough away so that their reputation won't follow them. If their prayer is answered and deliverance comes, invariably one spouse will say to the other, "If you breathe a word of how active we were in our former parish, I'll spread the word that you have a mental problem which causes you to hallucinate, imagining things that never occurred."

Parishioners in the Dark Can't Affirm Staff

In virtually all parishes, the parishioners have absolutely no idea how many different areas of individual ministry, programs, ministry teams, organizations, boards, councils, etc., exist. They don't know, of course, because they have never been told. Consequently, rather than being affirmed and congratulated for at least trying to do so many different things, staff members more typically experience complaints, comparisons and concern about what they are not doing adequately, or at all. Some say "Why aren't the priests playing basketball with the boys the way Father So-and-So did?" or "Why don't we ever see the staff at our social functions the way we used to?" And so on! Over-extended and overly-committed, the staff hears one complaint after another. Parishioners not only have the right to know how staff time is allocated; they have a right to contribute to the discernment which weighs alternative pastoral strategies affecting what they can expect of staff and what staff can expect from them. (However, only staff leadership makes the final decisions which shape the pastoral plan—the parish strategy and individual staff roles.) How staff time is allocated ultimately determines whether or not laity have access to ministry, support for and authority to conduct their ministry and promise of a fair distribution of ministerial responsibility, appreciating the limitation of any one person or family.

In my experience, many laity are as much or more concerned about the lack of opportunity to help their leadership engage these tensions or be informed of the decisions as they are about being informed regarding the utilization of parish money.

Most parish staff, particularly ordained priests, are genuinely hurt that most parishioners talk as if they believe that their leadership is basically lazy and has little to do. It is true that parish staff deserve the presumption that they work hard, but it is equally true that parishioners deserve to know what these hard days consist of.

Staff in the Dark Can't Affirm Staff

Furthermore, most staff members, prior to facing these questions and tensions together, have historically determined their respective roles and responsibilities alone, unilaterally and without adequate accountability, each deciding individually what to do, how to do it and how much time was sufficient to devote to it. Because of this pervasive unaccountability, I find, again and again, individual staff who feel as if they don't count. Not only are they not affirmed and more usually criticized by parishioners, but they often feel as if they don't count in the eyes and in the opinions of their fellow staff. The fact is that usually staff members simply do not know what each is doing and how each is devoting his or her respective time.

This reality, more than any other, ultimately is the source of discontent among parishioners about what staff members are doing and how they are utilizing their time. Individual parish staff have numerous, less than subtle ways of letting parishioners know that they haven't the slightest idea what the others are doing. Such total independence and lack of mutual accountability within a parish staff is a scandal in the eyes of parishioners.

Mutual Accountability a Relief for Staff

Evaluating and developing what a staff is doing individually and collectively, through a process providing mutual accountability, is a tremendous relief for parish staff. With assistance from their colleagues, staff need and want to have their roles shaped by the parish vision. They both want and need to feel accountable, to feel and to experience their colleagues as counting on them and viewing their ministry as important for the accomplishment of an overall pastoral plan.

Too frequently, the "fringe benefit" rewarding celibacy or a decision to accept a comparatively low-salaried parish staff position by a non-celibate has been the "freedom" to shape one's own role independently, with virtually no accountability. This so-called "fringe benefit" in the long run is most debasing, for it is a terrible experience to live with the uncertainty and lack of affirmation that one's life matters and counts from the collective perspective.

Pastoral Planning and Second Order Change

Pastoral planning must seriously consider the individual and collective limitations of ordained and non-ordained staff. Thus, changes in the pastoral plan to ensure more effective ministry in light of a parish's vision must provide an opportunity for unbundling (attenuating or eliminating) existing components of the pastoral plan in order to do something new. Alone, parish staff seem powerless and incapable of reducing their commitment and therefore the time given to any area of parish ministry. Staff need one another to learn how to say "No." Furthermore, such pastoral planning, with its choices and tensions, should include and involve at least the council, other parish leaders, and perhaps even a larger segment of the parish. The task of eliminating or attenuating a component of the pastoral plan is extremely difficult, because it is almost never a matter of setting aside something bad; rather, it is a matter of having to choose the best of alternatives. Second order change is impossible without a parish vision, but even with a vision it's difficult to walk away from something good. We like to keep our options open, avoiding the criticism that we are too narrow. Greatness is always accused of being too narrow!

No Universal Plan

There is no universal, terrific pastoral plan or parish strategy. The amount of individual and collective staff time which should be devoted to the existing or new components comprising the four major areas of a parish's pastoral plan will depend upon the unique characteristics of the parish and its vision—the gap it's trying to close between where it *is* and where it *is called to be*! It is, however, extremely important that a parish and its staff evaluate and develop what the parish (and therefore the staff) is doing, individually and collectively, to ensure more effective ministry in the light of the parish vision.

This evaluation and decision-making process requires discernment, but it is not necessary to expand the process by including as many people as were involved in the discernment of vision. It is, however, important to include at least parish leaders (and potential leaders), and to acquaint others of the results. Frequently, laity participating in this discernment process will encourage the pastor and other staff to forge ahead with courage to embrace new components of the pastoral plan called forth by the parish vision.

My experience in working with parishes to develop their pastoral plan has consistently demonstrated a need for the following:

1. *Call to Ministry:* experiences that affirm the gifts of people and call them to ministry, e.g., "Christ Renews His Parish," Cleveland, Ohio.

2. *Faith Sharing Groups:* experiences for small group faith-sharing opportunities which provide mutual ministry, support and nurture outreach, e.g., "Renew," Newark, New Jersey.

3. *Like-to-Like Ministry Teams:* experiences that provide support, faith-sharing and the opportunity to engage ethical and Christian principles for those sharing similar and secular careers.

4. *Parish Ministry Teams:* experiences that select, empower, enrich and support those ministering in parish ministry teams.

5. *Parish Leadership Development:* on-going enrichment and support for those people assuming the responsibility for pastoral leadership in the parish.

Concluding Remarks

The reward for evaluating and developing *what* a parish and its staff are doing, individually and collectively, to ensure more effective ministry in light of its parish vision is a sense of peace. Struggling with these issues and arriving at responsible decisions cannot and will not yield the same uplifting sense of great joy, born out of rediscovering who and why we are—the parish vision.

Pastoral planning is work, very noble and worthwhile. There is always the temptation to proclaim just the dream and remain on the top of the mountain, continually tasting its joy. If the parish succumbs to this temptation, the dream can't walk, and, if it can't walk, it can't keep pace with him who walks with and in front of us.

Chapter Five
The Predictable Evolution of Structures

A fundamental concern of the Church is governance, particularly how to establish structures for effective communication, accountability, pastoral leadership and decision-making. The ideals of the Second Vatican Council are yet to be realized because the dynamics of the legislative and administrative processes have not been understood and because obsolete structures have impeded implementation. Laity, clergy and bishops alike need to be informed of the art and science of governance. We need new and better processes for formulating policy, solving problems, making decisions, shaping organizations, maintaining communication, resolving conflict, deploying personnel and establishing norms. Present structures should be evaluated to determine their effectiveness. Where necessary, new structures must be designed.

For some time now, parishes and pastors have struggled with the development of new structures for communication, delegation of authority, shared responsibility and accountability. This struggle is not simply based on the need to discover new structures. The struggle often involves the more fundamental and cloaked issues of pastoral authority and subsidiarity versus collegiality. What was heard most clearly and somewhat myopically from the Second Vatican Council was the much needed emphasis on co-responsibility, as authority in the Church prior to Vatican II was and is most often remembered as authoritarian, unilateral and arbitrary.

Vatican II created a thaw in the freeze on Church structures created by Vatican I. This thaw was so sudden that it caused a flood of questions and an avalanche of confusion and reactions. The council itself did not redefine authority in the context of what it was calling forth from the whole Church, but placed it squarely in the perspective of those elements to which it is historically bound—the subsidiarity and collegiality of bishops.

In order to understand the changing relationship between authority and subsidiarity on the one hand and collegiality on the other, in the context of alternative structures for communication, accountability, pastoral leadership and decision-making, one must understand the predictable but normal development and changing structures that occur in any complex, organized social endeavor. The challenge to renew structures in today's parish can be fully appreciated only if one understands that all organized human endeavors, including parishes and dioceses, have a beginning, a period of growth and maturation, a peak period, followed by ossification and decline, preceding structural confusion and chaos. In parishes, as in other organizations, these stages or movements are accompanied by significant structural changes, reflecting and drastically altering the power and effectiveness of communication, accountability and the exercise of authority. Indeed, even the meaning of authority changes as structures evolve from one stage to the next. The last ten years have seen far too much unnecessary pain and too much careless and irresponsible experimentation with structures which could have been avoided by familiarity with these stages.

Authority of Person, Issue and Role

Before proceeding to describe the developmental stages and gaining an understanding and appreciation for the changing meaning of authority, subsidiarity and collegiality and the evolving relationships within these three principles, accompanied by different structures, it is necessary to distinguish initially three different kinds of authority: authority of *person*, authority of *issue* and authority of *role*.

1. *Authority of person* is the authority each brings to a situation by virtue of his or her own

unique personhood. Authority of person is that authority with which a person speaks by virtue of his or her reputation, regarding sincerity, integrity, responsibility, honesty, ability to be trusted, etc. Therefore, people who have the experience of belonging to many different groups, being present at many different kinds of gatherings, and attending various meetings often experience that in some groups their authority as a person is much greater than in others. In some groups their stock as a person is quite high, so when they speak, everyone listens. In other groups where their stock is quite low, what they say seems to matter little.

2. *Authority of issue* is authority that a person can bring to any situation by virtue of his or her special knowledge, skills, experience, training and credentials. Even a person with low authority of person in a group knows that moment when he or she can speak with "special authority" because everyone knows that he or she has special knowledge, skills, training, experiences or credentials with regard to the issue at hand.

3. *Authority of role* is that authority given deference and recognized by virtue of a particular responsibility which a person embodies in a complex social endeavor requiring different roles. Authority of role is derived from having a particular role in a social endeavor requiring structure. Authority of role cannot be separated from structure because it derives its meaning from that structure. It is the authority that a person speaks with by virtue of his or her responsibility within an organized human endeavor.

It is *authority of role* that requires an examination of the relationship between authority, subsidiarity and collegiality in the context of changing organizational structures. The meaning of these three principles of Church governance and the nature of their relationship changes, depending upon the structure in which they are exercised. To understand this, let us consider what typically happens to structures in the developmental and changing stages of a complex social endeavor during founding, growth, maturation, peak, ossification and decline.

The Time of Inception—Beginning—Founding

Usually, the beginning of most Catholic parishes, like most organized human endeavors, is a totally collegial process. A group of people come together and begin to talk and dream about accomplishing something they cannot possibly accomplish alone. In the very beginning, all they have is their dream and each other. They know why they are gathering to meet, to plan, to hope, beginning with only the slightest idea of what they are going to do and how they are going to do it.

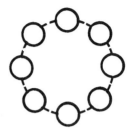

There is no structural differentiation and no differences among them in terms of authority of role. There is no subsidiarity in deference to role authority. Any differences in authority among the people involved are matters of authority of person or authority of issue. In time, the opinions of some will be held in higher regard than the opinions of others. The ability to speak with authority on a particular issue will vary, depending on how respective life experiences, training, skills and special knowledge provide each with the credibility to speak to an issue.

The people involved in the founding of a parish or any other essentially collective endeavor begin their enterprise as colleagues. The only principle of governance is collegiality. As colleagues, they first meet informally and irregularly, and then more regularly and formally, dreaming and talking together about why their endeavor is needed.

They struggle to discover and prepare to announce their unity of purpose, shared vision, hopes, dreams and aspirations. They share in faith the conviction that each has a part of the truth; they grow in their commitment to allow one another's experience to change and influence them. Together they become capable, competent and confident to articulate and announce the vision which provides the foundation for their "common-union" (communion). They grow in courage to call one another forth and to be called forth by one another to do all that love requires to fulfill that vision, supporting each other in the quest.

Most parishes begin this way, but so also do most collective endeavors: schools, hospitals, law firms, industrial enterprises—all kinds of human enterprise.

Leadership and Structure Are Born

However, as talking and dreaming lead to more concerted action and membership grows, it becomes increasingly difficult and then impossible to govern solely on the basis of collegiality. At this point, in most human endeavors, organization begins. A leader is selected either from within or from without, one who did not participate in the initial struggles. In the history of many parishes, it is at this point that the founding group petitions the diocese to send a leader. Frequently, in recent years, someone is sent by the diocese to an area ripe for the founding of a new parish, confronted with the initial challenge of forming a small group of people to share that dream.

Whichever way structure begins and leadership emerges, a dynamic is created by the complementary relationship between the leader's role authority and the founding group's experience of collegiality.

Soon someone from the founding group will inhale a deep breath, issuing the following mandate, conditions and terms, before pausing for the second breath: "We can't go on meeting as we have, making every decision together. We need someone to lead us. If you will be our leader, we will follow you. We will stand behind you. We will support you. We will take direction from you, *but* if you dare to try to take us someplace we don't want to go, if you are not faithful to our dream, we will begin slicing, we will begin cutting away our fidelity to your authority, starting at your toes, working our way past your ankles, up to your knees and we won't stop there." There is a sigh, a pause, and the group takes its next breath.

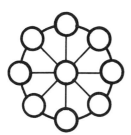

The leader soon realizes that his *authority of role* and *responsibility* is not to reside "on top" of others but in the center of their essentially collective endeavor. He or she will be a servant to the group; he or she soon learns that his or her responsibility is to continue to author, give birth to and guarantee collegiality among the others. If effective collegiality occurs and bears the continuing fruit of collective aspirations, he or she will continue to be an effective leader. If the leader is remiss in authoring and guaranteeing this collegiality, collective values and aspirations become unclear, the vision dims and the leader will begin to experience the fact that his or her authority is growing weak and dissipating.

The founding group soon learns that they must be faithful to their promise of subsidiarity and maintain continuing fidelity to one another through the exercise of collegiality in order to author, empower, guarantee and ensure an effective leader.

Thus in the historical growth and development of every parish there is that period shortly toward the end of its founding during which everyone involved has the lived, first-hand experience and appreciation that it is effective collegiality which authors, empowers and guarantees effective authority. In the most basic sense, the principles of collegiality, authority and subsidiarity are interdependent and complementary. They effectively author one another.

This lived experience of the principle of complementarity between role authority and the promise of subsidiarity on the one hand and the experience of and necessity for on-going collegiality on the other forms the fundamental principle for expanding structures in the next stage in the development of this essentially collective enterprise. It is worthwhile pausing to appreciate fully that these three principles of governing are complementary in the fullest sense of the word. "You can't have one without the other(s)," as the song says!

It would make no sense whatsoever to this leader or this group if someone were to ask, "Are you going to run this parish collegially or authoritatively?" Such a question would sound as silly as suggesting the word "men" if among all people there weren't any women, or "fathers" and "mothers" if there were no children. It's extremely important to understand and appreciate that there was a moment in the history of founding every parish, every diocese, every collective human endeavor when that question would sound utterly foolish, ridiculous and absurd. Why is that question asked so frequently today?

Maturation

If a complex human endeavor becomes successful, the number of people involved, of course, will grow. It ceases to be the enterprise of the small group and their leader and becomes an "organization." It might even become multi-national and need to contend with great physical distances, languages and cultural differences. Although the behavior of several hundred, perhaps even several thousand people, will need to be coordinated, it will become impossible for all to communicate with each other. Parishes, like other organizations, simply become too large to permit face-to-face communication as the mechanism of coordination.

In parishes, division of labor will evolve, requiring considerable interdependence and, therefore, coordination among groups. During the stage of maturation, the major organizational problem is to create the best possible structure for coordinating and integrating efforts among and between the various groups. A good deal of information must be processed, to coordinate these interdependent groups, which necessitates the emergence of a complex authority structure. Middle management is born and must learn to live in the creative tension of representing central role authority to peripheral groups and vice versa. During this stage of maturation, parishes will grow and evolve and structures will emerge keenly sensitive to the importance of centrality and the value of authority in an essentially collective enterprise. During this stage they remember, understand, and develop structures which reflect their continued appreciation for authority's role in authoring, empowering and guaranteeing effective collegiality and vice versa. Structures will evolve different responsibility and authority roles. Role authority will differ among persons within this structure depending upon their centrality in this essentially collective enterprise, but the structure will always reverence the need for communication and accountability to flow into and out of the center with equivalent intensity. Communication is in both directions, accountability is mutual, and the authority and power of those in the center authors a greater sense of the authority and power of those with responsibilities at the periphery. Similarly the power and authority of those at the periphery undergirds, authors and guarantees the authority of those at the center.

Power is viewed as a fact of life, and, as such, neither good nor bad. It is viewed as corporate property. In other words, power belongs to the corporate body and not just to the individuals in whom it is embodied. Power is seen as mutual. People called to accept certain responsibilities are given the necessary authority. Others commit themselves to leadership which is the exercise of subsidiarity. Both honor their commitments, realizing that to negate the authority of the other means to negate one's own authority. Everyone makes a concerted effort to support those with more central role authority so that their authority can be of service to the corporate body. Responsible people do not try to render others powerless but hold them accountable to operate, openly responsive to the needs and aspirations of the corporate body.

Structure serves to help center communication, accountability, responsibility, subsidiarity, authority and collegiality. Structure is not merely a structure of differential role authority. *It is the same structure that determines where, how, and among whom collegiality must occur.* The structure shows where authority is responsible for seeing that collegiality occurs within groups, between groups, and between persons responsible for coordination of various groups. *No one is on top of anyone.* There exist only differences in role authority relative to the structure for centering communication, responsibility, authority, accountability and collegiality for the sake of the corporate body. At this stage the organization is *most* purposive and the relationship of authority, subsidiarity and collegiality is *most* complementary.

Ossification—Hierarchy

There is a moment in the historical development of all collective human endeavors, including parishes and dioceses, when at the peak of their vitality everyone succumbs to the human temptation to chisel the "winning strategy" in marble. The organization begins the process of routinizing what it is doing. The memory of why, and the purpose for which it is doing these things, vision and dream, gradually begin to fade.

This is the time in the historical development of organizations, and therefore in the life of a parish or diocese, when subtle changes begin and are soon accompanied by substantial change in organizational structures. There emerges an uncertainty, ambiguity or sense of rigidity regarding collective purpose and values. Authority becomes lax in its responsibility to author, guarantee, and empower effective collegiality, and various groups of people with different responsibilities cease to hold those with role authority mutually accountable. Soon those with role authority cease to count. Authority and subsidiarity, which provided stability for organizational operations during the "centrality phase," become ends in themselves rather than means to an end. As uncertainty increases and complementarity between central authority and peripheral aspirations diminishes, many "middle management" roles and responsibilities disappear. Hierarchy is born.

Authority is viewed and arranged in a vertical hierarchy of power. In parishes, virtually every decision of substance, even the simple and insignificant, is referred directly to the pastor who soon becomes overloaded. Every situation for which there is no pre-planned response must be referred upward. Soon almost everyone demands direct access to the pastor who becomes overloaded and overwhelmed, and eventually begins to act unilaterally and arbitrarily. Serious delays develop between the upward

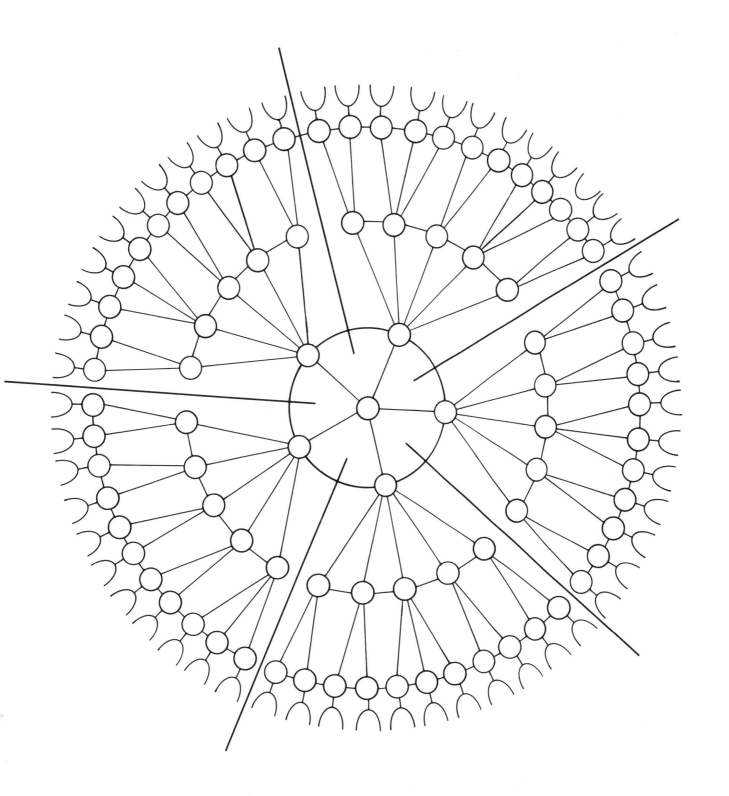

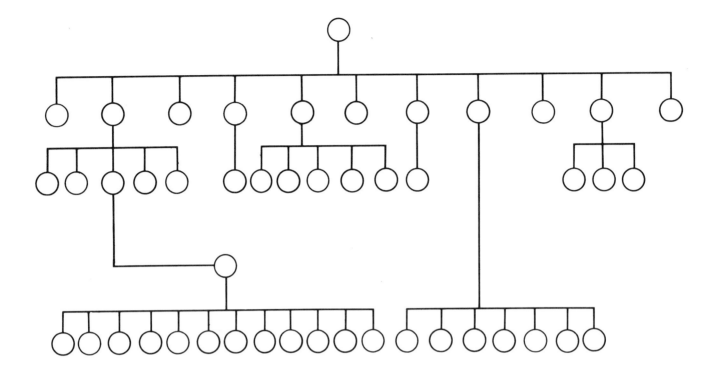

transmission of information and the response to the information downward. Authority and power cease to be experienced as corporate. After a time, hierarchy is employed *instead of* rather than *in addition to* middle management. Peripheral authority and the collegiality which empowers and guarantees other authority is dissipated. If collegiality occurs at all, it is only experienced at the summit of a hierarchy among those few within the organization attributed as having any power at all. People at the bottom of a hierarchy have no power, no authority and nothing to offer. Authority is no longer authored, empowered, guaranteed or derived to any extent from the exercise of collegiality among those at the periphery in an essentially collective enterprise. Instead, authority is viewed as derived exclusively from a "higher power." Relationships between what were formally experienced as a great people and their leaders shift from being mutually supportive to competitive. Leaders become bosses and the bossed become nothing. In a hierarchical structure one begins to feel as if the very nature of the structure is screaming to the parishioners, "Remember, I'm the boss; you're nothing," to which the parishioners reply, "Big deal—boss over nothing!"

People become testy, jealous and angered by the authority which claims the right to rule without communication and accountability, operative in both directions. Saddened, but happily at the same time, people actually begin to enjoy watching au-

thority fail as they stand at the bottom of a new hierarchically arranged structure. They begin to feel or even say to themselves and to one another, "The higher the monkey climbs the ladder, the better you see his ass."

Many human enterprises which accrue money and pay salaries can and do survive in this stage for a long time, utilizing scientific management procedures that yield the most effective results possible within hierarchical structures. They can sustain themselves in this phase because they pay salaries to maintain commitment to their enterprise. Even so, they recognize the loss of the efficiency, vitality, sense of purpose and enthusiasm which characterized their endeavor when structures were based on centrality. Even salaries, however, do not insulate from decline into the next stage—trough. The Catholic parish, unlike an organization which pays salaries to all who contribute to its endeavor, obviously, is not capable of sustaining itself in this phase before rapidly beginning to decline.

Decline and Death—The Trough

Most Catholic parishes have experienced a "liberation phenomenon," an informal, often inarticulated, declaration of independence. People have withdrawn their investment in persons with "higher" (previously more central) authority. Seemingly, all organizational structure has disappeared, with the parish being reimaged as a "community." Such

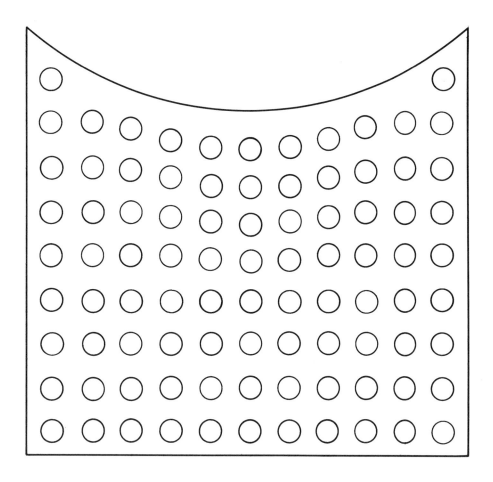

an image usually is structureless and seems to imply that a parish can operate like a small group of five hundred to ten thousand people. Rules for organizational operation have ceased to have meaning. There are virtually no rights or wrongs in the service of organizational integrity.

Phillip Roth calls this stage the "organizational trough." Everyone exists within the boundaries of the organization without structures and without the benefit of effective authority or collegiality. The climate is highly person-centered. Everyone demands freedom. There is much more emphasis on personal fulfillment and "doing your own thing" than on addressing collective responsibilities and organizational problems. The norms that begin to dominate anticipated behavior are "If it feels good—do it!" and "I'm not in this world to live up to your expectations and you're not in this world to live up to mine. If we can work together, fine; if not, it can't be helped." Although this stage provides an initial sense of relief and liberation from the arbitrary and non-interdependent exercise of authority of hierarchical structure, its benefits are short-lived. In time people soon learn that the confusion and mayhem experienced in the trough are as difficult to cope with as the unilateral, arbitrary and autocratic characteristics of a hierarchy.

Concluding Remarks

This chapter has attempted to describe as clearly as possible the normal evolutionary structural changes experienced by any organization. This evolution is most apparent when one watches closely the changes occurring during the founding, growth, maturation, ossification and decline of a new contemporary parish. The stages of predictable changes occurring in the growth, maturation and decline of a contemporary corporate parish, of course, recapitulate the changes which occur in the universal Church of which the new parish is a part. In social systems this is equivalent to the biogenic law: "Ontogeny recapitulates phylogeny." In biology, this law refers to the fact that during the development of the individual, he or she passes through all of the evolutionary stages which gave birth to the different phyla. There was a time (intra-uterine) when each of us had gills, then a tail, etc.

What has been said in this chapter about hierarchical structures should not be construed as a criticism or an indictment of the episcopate. Some people refer, of course, to the episcopate as "the hierarchy." It will be clear to the reader, by the end of Chapter 7, that the author has the utmost respect and appreciation for the episcopacy. Therefore, I ask the reader's indulgence until the end of Chapter 7 before prematurely judging my attitude and regard for the episcopate. References to *a hierarchical structure* should not be construed to contain my feelings and attitudes toward what some people call "the hierarchy."

Chapter Six
What Happens to Centrality, Purposiveness and Presence?

Most people in Catholic parishes today exist oscillating between hierarchy and trough with only a dim memory of centrality. They believe, although falsely, that their only choice is between anarchy and hierarchy. Parish staffs and parishioners alike yearn for structures that center authority, delegate responsibility, provide mutual accountability and ensure better communication. In short, they yearn for structures that ensure complementarity within the principles of authority, subsidiarity and collegiality, wherein authority authors, empowers and guarantees effective collegiality and vice versa. Staff and parishioners alike seek an authority which calls forth and leads rather than legislates and bosses. However, the road to centrality with its complementarity between authority, subsidiarity and collegiality is made extremely difficult by the fact that people vividly remember the pain of hierarchy and don't want to get burned again. Often, attempts to introduce new structures for organizational integrity are perceived solely as an attempt to revive unilateral and arbitrary hierarchical structures.

What Happens Initially To Cause the Move from Centrality to Hierarchy?

Very frequently when the stages of evolving structures are presented there is an immediate sense of finally understanding and appreciating something very important which priests, religious and laity have felt but couldn't articulate. Almost immediately someone will invariably raise his/her hand and ask, "What happens to cause the move from centrality to hierarchy in the first place?" It's an important question for two reasons. First, if cen-

trality structures are so powerful and capable of authoring the lived experience of organizational vitality and purposiveness, people want to know why they are abandoned for a less effective alternative? Second, it's important to understand why this change occurs in order to grasp how to develop centrality.

The Concept of Climate

Human groups and organizations are formed and exist to meet needs and to fulfill a purpose. Therefore, the "success" of any social endeavor can be measured in terms of the extent to which this is achieved. Large complex social organizations such as parishes or dioceses have at least two easily identifiable sets of needs: (1) task needs; (2) person needs.

Task needs are those requirements which are present as a function of the work that is to be done by the system. A parish, for example, needs to have adequate supplies and materials, properly trained personnel, appropriate physical facilities, sufficient funds to operate, input from parishioners and community, and plans and strategies for implementing programs.

Person needs are those needs present within a parish simply because human beings are present and active within it. These people, whether adults or children in a parish, bring with them needs associated with self-worth, for example the need for belonging, achievement, recognition, identity and integrity, as well as others such as financial security, etc. These person needs are of such a nature that they are met, to a greater or lesser degree, in the interactions between people within a parish.

Any broad change effort directed toward improving an organization's "success" of necessity focuses on:

1. Increasing the efficiency and effectiveness of the organization's task activities (i.e., better meeting the task needs).

2. Maximizing the possibility for human growth and development within the organization (i.e., better meeting the person needs).

In any organization there exist needs which are met by performing certain tasks and fostering human relationships. It is important to be aware that a wide spectrum of task and person needs may exist within a parish even though they may not be recognized as such by the organization's members or legitimized by the organization's structures. The extent to which these task and person needs are seen as important depends on a multitude of factors which are heavily influenced by the value priorities (value levels) inherent in the parish's philosophy and held by the parish's members.

In studying any social system there are *two primary dimensions* which are important in determining the success of the organization.

1. *Quality of Relationships.* In a social system such as a parish, a multitude of relationships are established and maintained between and among people. The quality of these relationships may vary from extremely superficial to very meaningful and/or very competitive to very supportive. The quality of the relationships established and maintained between and among individuals and groups significantly affects the potential for human growth and development within the parish.

Organizational processes which comprise quality of relationships include development of commitment, expression of ideas, expression of feelings, expression of values, management of differences and development of human resources.

2. *Quality of Directedness.* In a social system there is a myriad of task activities which must be planned, implemented, and evaluated in order for the system to function. The quality of directedness of these task activities may vary from aimless and random to being highly goal directed and synergistic. The degree to which the task activities are directed (i.e., are planned and implemented in light of clear organizational purpose) significantly affects the efficiency and effectiveness of the organization.

The organizational processes constituting quality of directedness include purpose clarification, goal generation, problem identification, problem-solving, decision-making, implementation and evaluation.

Types of Climate

The "climate" of an organization is the predominant feeling tone created by different emphasis, especially the effort to integrate quality of directedness and quality of relationships. The emphasis on either of these dimensions can be low, medium or high, and this emphasis, together with the effort attempting to integrate (or not integrate) them, determines the five climate types commonly found within organizations. Ultimately, organizational climate depends upon the relative value people within the organization place on quality of directedness and quality of relationships and their integration.

Routine Climate

The routine climate (L,L) is characterized by *random, aimless, apathetic* and *impersonal* work activities. Peer relationships are generally marked by *distrust, fear, insecurity, competitiveness, hostility* and *threat.* People in authority or leadership positions are generally viewed with suspicion, jealousy and fear. The work itself in this (routine) climate is generally approached in a non-committed, apathetic manner and is seen as non-challenging, meaningless and worthy of little more than "going through the motions." It must be pointed out that not all personnel will react to this climate in this manner. For many people, this climate will be one that is relatively "safe," requiring little investment on their part, and this makes it even more appealing to them. Efforts to change this climate will be welcomed by many people and yet seen as "rocking the boat" by others.

Task Directed Climate

A theme for the task directed climate is often "get the work done *right* the first time." This (H,L) climate is characterized by high systematic and regulated work activities constantly evaluated in terms of efficiency and effectiveness. There is generally much control exercised over when and how a task is to be accomplished, with emphasis on uniformity and consistency. The emphasis in this climate is on acquisition and application of highly polished skills required to "reach the goals."

People in this (H,L) climate generally feel the job they are doing is important and derive most of their satisfaction from doing the job well. In this climate, a person's worth is very much related to his

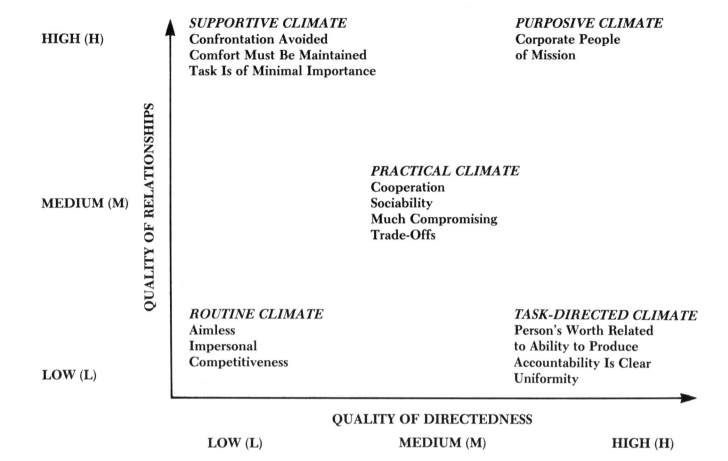

HIGH (H)

SUPPORTIVE CLIMATE
Confrontation Avoided
Comfort Must Be Maintained
Task Is of Minimal Importance

PURPOSIVE CLIMATE
Corporate People
of Mission

QUALITY OF RELATIONSHIPS

MEDIUM (M)

PRACTICAL CLIMATE
Cooperation
Sociability
Much Compromising
Trade-Offs

LOW (L)

ROUTINE CLIMATE
Aimless
Impersonal
Competitiveness

TASK-DIRECTED CLIMATE
Person's Worth Related
to Ability to Produce
Accountability Is Clear
Uniformity

QUALITY OF DIRECTEDNESS

LOW (L)   MEDIUM (M)   HIGH (H)

level of skill and job proficiency, i.e., a person's "status in the organization is very much related to his ability to produce." The emphasis on production in this climate often leads to competition among people which leaves them feeling isolated and fearing disapproval and rejection for making mistakes. These feelings often lead people to be more secretive and less likely to share with one another.

Supportive Climate

The (L,H) supportive climate is one which is characterized by exchanges of warmth, sympathy and concern between members. In this climate, since there is often an overriding concern about "hurting a person's feelings," interpersonal conflict and confrontation are usually minimized or avoided, in an effort to foster and maintain cohesion. People in this climate generally respond to each other as equals with very little formality involved in the relationship, i.e., differences in skill level, education, competencies, roles, etc., are minimized.

Task requirements and activities are of minimal importance in the (L,H) climate and are often felt as intrusions which threaten cohesion. The major focus

of any evaluational activities conducted in this climate is on the satisfaction of the members as they perform the tasks. If some dissatisfaction is felt on the part of someone, efforts are generally directed toward changing the nature of the task to fit the satisfaction needs of the individual rather than focus on what is required by the task and placing demands on the individual to change.

Practical Climate

The (M,M) practical climate is characterized by cooperation and sociability, i.e., relationships are maintained at a level which allows people to negotiate with each other, make trade-offs as to who will do what, and in general, make compromises that leave most people feeling fairly good while an adequate job gets done. What is important in this climate is that everyone identifies what he wants to do and then structures the work accordingly. This requires that some people may get "bent a little out of shape" (i.e., take on an assignment they would prefer to do without) but through bargaining and trade-offs (e.g., be able to devote one-half of the time to a favorite project even though it may not be directly

53

related to the organization's goals) an amenable settlement of some sort is made. In this climate, conflict is seen as a "fact of life" that is often the responsibility of an individual to resolve unless most of the organization members are affected by the conflict. If most people are affected by some sort of conflict or stress, then they will generally work together to resolve it. If not, an individual (or coalition of individuals) usually must develop some bargain that makes a change in others attractive enough for them to change. This kind of "federation" often permits the development of a few close relationships among scattered small groups of individuals within the organization and people quite often identify much more with this tight peer group than they do with the total organization. These small pockets of vested interests require that people maintain enough contact with each other to know what others are doing and yet feel a need for sufficient distance to maintain a strong bargaining position whenever and with whomever it may be required.

Purposive Climate

The (H,H) purposive climate is characterized by member activity which is highly oriented to corporate purpose and open to shared evaluation and influence. Organizational members have a strong sense of common purpose and have developed and act on a strong commitment to that purpose *and* to each other, i.e., there is a strong commitment to integrate the needs of the organization with the needs of the organization's members.

Acting out of this shared sense of purpose, people in this climate are able to challenge each other openly, value differences among themselves as a strength rather than a threat to cohesion, and support and learn from each other without the fear of being seen as somehow weak or incompetent. Tension and conflict situations are perceived as opportunities to be confronted with vigor in order to grow rather than to be avoided. Evaluation of both interpersonal and task competencies is valued as a way to increase the integration of both (in individuals and as an organization).

People generally experience a purposive climate as exciting and meaningful, as freeing and yet very demanding. They often experience cycles of agreement and disagreement between and among organizational members which, rather than being threatening, leave people with a sense of potency and respect for themselves and each other.

Not all people will experience a purposive climate as exhilarating and growthful. The demands to

integrate a focus on *task* and *person* needs can be overwhelming to many people, especially if they are moving into a purposive climate from a long and relatively satisfying experience in either a supportive (L,H) or task-directed (H,L) climate. The necessity for people to be open about their own aspirations, relative to the organization's purpose, to be open to feedback from others regarding their learning needs and the responsibility which comes with interdependence, is often more than some people feel ready or able to do. However, in this climate, mutual support of each other and a growing sense of common purpose help the personal relationships and task activities to take on more meaning and a greater sense of integration. It is in this climate that people can begin to take a greater pride in both the quality of their relationships with each other and the quality of what it is that they produce together.

The Shift in Organizational Climate Toward Routinization

There are two paths that a purposive organization, a corporate people of mission, can follow to deterioration, death and ruin. The path followed most frequently by the Catholic parish and diocese is that created by an initial and more intense devaluation of quality of relationships. Later, quality of directedness begins to lose value also, but that is much slower and more subtle.

I don't mean by this that a church wakes up one day and says, "Let's put less value on the quality of relationships!" What actually happens is, of course, more positively motivated. Feeling themselves at the pinnacle of success, people naturally try to routinize "winning strategy." New questions, new ideas, and conflict about how to do things are naturally viewed as a waste of time. People should learn the tried and true.

The local Catholic church usually begins its descent from purposiveness in a burst of task-directed activity, sliding down the low path (see preceding diagram) to aimless, impersonal routinization. They pass through a stage where anybody's and everybody's worth is related to his or her ability to produce.

Evidence that deterioration to routinization follows the lower path (see preceding diagram) is readily apparent, watching what happens when these parishes begin to smell the odor of death and dying. There is a burst of activity to rediscover purposiveness by following the high path of emphasizing quality of relationships, with a total disregard for the quality of directedness. At the pinnacle of this

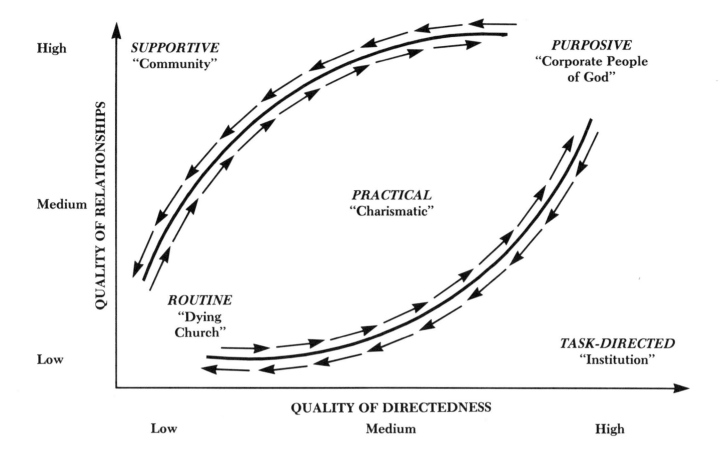

High   *SUPPORTIVE*   *PURPOSIVE*

"Community"   "Corporate People of God"

PRACTICAL "Charismatic"

ROUTINE "Dying Church"

TASK-DIRECTED "Institution"

QUALITY OF RELATIONSHIPS

Medium

Low

QUALITY OF DIRECTEDNESS

Low   Medium   High

activity, all values are aimed at personal growth, appreciating individual strengths and weaknesses, personal freedom, avoiding conflict and obtaining personal comfort, at any cost.

It isn't Catholic leadership alone nor is it the Catholic people alone who try to chisel "the winning strategy" in granite, venerating routinization. It is both. It is everyone. It is done for the right reasons—we think. It is a natural and predictable error.

The Structural Shift from Centrality to Hierarchy

At some point in time, parishes following the low path of regression from purposiveness to routinization gradually come to view a hierarchy as a more attractive and more effective alternative structure. These parishes know *what* they want and that their leadership can do it best. There is no need to talk anymore, to dream together, to face up to differences. In short, there is no need to be collegial. Collegiality becomes part of that quality of relationship stuff that is time-wasting.

Catholic leadership does not steal the opportunity of collegiality from the Catholic people; both agree it is unnecessary. Since it is no longer needed, those in authority can, we reason, expand their span of direct influence and control. All pastors in a diocese become directly accountable to the ordinary, since there is no longer any need for him to foster their collegiality for discerning and deciding purpose, declared objectives, desired outcome and "how to do it." Furthermore, there no longer is a need for supervising and supporting pastors. In a parish, anyone and everyone with responsibility or even a mere query has direct access to the pastor.

Initially, the decision to abandon structures for centrality in order to adopt hierarchical structures is well reasoned and well motivated. Of course, no one argues for the value of unilateral, arbitrary, unaccountable and authoritarian leadership. It is much later, after designing and embracing hierarchical structures, overloading the span of control, dissipating collegiality and placing impossible demands on our leadership, that we begin to yell, "Arbitrary! Unilateral! Authoritarian!"

It is easier to blame the leaders, describing them in these terms, than to resume responsible collegiality. How abandoned, lonely and embittered these leaders must feel, put by us way up on a pedestal, where we can all take an easy shot.

Levels of Presence

Human communication involves a complex set of exchanges often difficult to study and describe. Attempts to improve these exchanges require a conceptual framework in which to view the content of the exchange (i.e., what gets communicated) and also the process of the exchange (i.e., how the communication is made). One way to view the communication process between people is in terms of the quality of presence that people bring to the communication situation. Quality of presence can be thought of as the degree to which people engage one another as they communicate. The remainder of this section will attempt to describe six different levels of presence. More complex levels of presence necessarily incorporate the attributes of the earlier levels.

1. *Symbolic Presence.* At this level we find the most passive presence in which a person simply observes the appearance of another, making judgments and searching for the meaning of these external appearances. Obvious examples of symbolic presence are a police uniform, a clerical collar, the striped clothing of a prison inmate and the habit. Frequently, the person wishing to communicate through symbolic presence desires to utilize the subconscious meaning of things such as color, fire and water. This unleashing of pre-conscious symbolic meaning is frequently misconstrued as capturing the essence and therefore the highest level of communication and common-union.

2. *Attentiveness.* At this level we find a passive presence in which one person observes and listens to another. Words and ideas are heard; signs of emotion and feeling are observed. Behavior is carefully observed, but there is very little exchange. The speaker in this case will often experience this passive presence in the other person as showing him to be remote, detached, uninvolved and indifferent. Even though the listener is present and seeing and hearing, there is no reciprocity or "giving back." There is a taking but not a giving by the listener. The exchange is simply one way.

This level of presence leaves the speaker not knowing if what he is saying is being understood or if how he is feeling about what he is saying is being picked up by the listener. In a sense, the speaker has no way of knowing what parts of what he is saying are being picked up by the listener. In addition, the speaker has no way of knowing what the listener is doing with the message that is picked up. Is it being interpreted and evaluated? If so, what sort of interpretation is the person making? If it is being evaluated, what are the criteria? The speaker has no way of knowing; he experiences the listener as "playing his cards *very* close to his chest."

The listener, on the other hand, because of the passive level of presence, has no way of knowing if he has accurately captured the *meaning* of what the speaker is intending to convey. Instead, all judgments and interpretations remain private and are not checked out. Here again we see that the exchange is minimal and subject to inordinate distortion, error and misunderstanding.

3. *Understanding.* Here we go beyond "paying attention" and take a more active stance toward being present to each other. Here each person listens for more than ideas and attempts to capture the *meaning* of what the other is attempting to communicate. We listen actively in an attempt to understand not just ideas and content but the person. We try, through questioning, to understand the feelings, values, meaning and importance of the ideas to the other person. However, a listener in this situation may be experienced by the speaker as (1) a counselor or therapist who is only interested in understanding him or her, and (2) being "one up," i.e., the listener knows about the speaker yet the speaker knows very little about the listener. Again, we have minimal *mutual exchange* because this is still primarily one-way communication.

4. *Responding.* As another person expresses himself or herself we are affected by it to a greater or lesser degree. We have ideas, feelings, etc., in reaction to that person, his or her expression, or the implications of his or her communication. At this level (responding), we both *listen* to the other as well as react to the other's expression. We listen receptively, i.e., we let the other's statements and feelings affect us emotionally. We let him or her in. We also share our reactions and responses to what he or she is communicating—he or she knows "where we are". We identify areas of agreement and disagreement. We have dialogued. We have responded to each other. However, even though we have identified and clarified agreements and differences, this is as far as it goes. There is no real commitment to pursuing the issues or differences further, i.e., it is enough that they are clarified and now it is up to each person *individually* to pursue any implications the differences may have. This kind of an exchange

often leaves people feeling heard and understood and yet wondering, "Is that all there is?"

5. *Committed Responding.* As adults and brothers and sisters in the Lord, we have an obligation to go beyond simply clarifying differences. None of us can assume that because there are differences one of us is "right" and the other "wrong." This stance leaves out the opportunity for each person to learn from the other, especially in the shared experiences of faith.

Instead, if people can approach differences as being a function of each person's having a "piece of the truth" then between them they have a larger "slice of truth" than individually. When this occurs, we see people *committed* to the experience of the other person, engaging and exploring in faith *together.* In this situation, each person allows the other to influence and change him or her. There is a commitment to being open to this mutually influencing process. People respond to each other out of that common commitment.

I am called to share in faith. Your experience has implications for me and I am committed to letting your experience change and influence me just as you are committed to letting mine influence you. We are beyond communication and in communion.

6. *Calling and Being Called.* In recognizing our mutual commitment to each other's faith experience, we come to a greater understanding of what it is that we are both committed to live and work together to accomplish. As we discern together, we also evaluate our common efforts. We are in a position to affirm those areas in which we both (or individually) have moved on our commitment to a common vision and to identify those areas where we both (or individually) may have fallen short.

In this process, out of a mutual faith commitment, we are able to challenge one another to move more vigorously to meet our commitments and to provide the support to each other that is required in tackling hard problems together.

At this level of communication we do more than dialogue; we move on a commitment to help each other grow and develop in the Lord.

In sharing each other's experience, we clarify the common faith as the center of our experience. Together we recognize the vision to which we are called and the ways in which we *are* and *are not* living up to that vision. Hence, we let each other call us to that vision and support each other in the quest. (See summary diagram of the Six Levels of Presence.)

Regression in Levels of Presence in Hierarchical Structures

Abandoning collegiality devalues the quality of relationships, exchanges centrality for hierarchy and so ossifies existing means to achieve purpose. No longer do we unceasingly explore our vision, our purpose and our dream. The foundation crumbles that provides for high levels of presence, "common-union" (communion) and "common-unity" (community).

In short, our memories dull and we forget why we were ever doing what we were once hell-bent to achieve. This condition is like getting on an airplane to go somewhere, not knowing why you're going. Presence dissipates as our dream and purpose dull, and the structures we are committed to block our capability to renew and rediscover our purpose, our excitement and our dream. We can't call or be called forth by one another because we don't remember the vision that gives us the right and obligation to call and be called. Secondly, we lose the ability to respond to one another in a committed way as we no longer share the same faith vision. We can no longer feel committed to influence one another or be influenced by one another. When committed responding disappears, we lose "common-union" (communion).

All we have left is communication, and even in communication at its best all we can say to one another is, "I'm not in this world to live up to your expectations and you're not in this world to live up to mine. If we can work together—beautiful; if we don't, it can't be helped." But in time even communication diminishes. We say to one another, "Let there be spaces in our togetherness," and "If it feels good, do it."

Our communication regresses from responding presence to understanding presence to attentive presence until finally only symbolic communication is left. We communicate by watching, not listening or talking. Even some symbolic actions representative of higher levels of presence are met with dissonant feelings of disgust, fright and excitement. Remember the confusion and ambivalence about the handshake of peace!

Concluding Remarks

What happens initially to cause the movement from centrality to a hierarchy helps us to understand and to evaluate the immense power of structures. Structures establish norms which hinder or promote differing organizational climates. Structures dictate the scope and depth of levels of pres-

SIX LEVELS OF PRESENCE

1 SYMBOLIC	"I am what I wear," e.g., habit, medals, police uniform, clerical collar
2 ATTENTIVE	I see you I hear you But I hold back any sharing of my ideas or feelings This may frustrate others around me
3 UNDERSTANDING	I hear you I ask questions for clarification I seek to understand your values, ideas, meaning and feelings But you may experience me as being "one up," i.e., knowing more about you than you do about me (therapeutic mode)
4 RESPONDING	I hear what you say I share my reactions so that you "know where I am" You and I have dialogued, we have mutually shared, but we are not committed to the experience of each other
5 COMMITTED RESPONDING	I am called to share in faith Your experience has implications for me and I am committed to letting your experience change and influence me just as you are committed to letting mine influence you We are beyond communication and in communion
6 CALLING AND BEING CALLED	In sharing each other's experience we clarify the common faith as the center of our experience Together we recognize the vision to which we are called and the ways in which we *are* and *are not* living up to that vision Hence, we let each other call us to that vision and support each other in the quest

ence, permitted and encouraged in the service of pastoral authority and collegiality.

Structures can't discern the Lord's dream for the people comprising the local church in a particular place at a particular time. However structures can inhibit and even prevent his people from discerning his vision. Chapter 7 presents a comparison of structural alternatives for the contemporary parish, evaluating these alternatives in light of the concepts discussed in this chapter.

Chapter Seven
The Heart of the Matter
of Structural Alternatives

After so many painful experiences in the Church in the last ten or fifteen years, it is now quite delightful that a basic intuition is being confirmed—the intuition that Church takes place among people, that the bulk of Christian experience, reflection, choice and action takes place in the parish, not in the upper structures of the Church, not in the movements. Rather, it either does happen or doesn't happen at the parochial level. Clergy in parish work no longer feel so inferior. It used to be nice and a great thing to be appointed to the seminary, but now it seems to be a nicer thing to be appointed from the seminary to a parish. We have some notion that this is important, that parish is *the* important place for Christian experience.

It Must Begin with Vision

Faith is not simply "completed in action" but for its very understanding must be found in the actions of a people struggling to discover and forge the meaning of their future and the shape of their destiny, always faithful to the wisdom of their heritage. Therefore, any structural change in a parish should be rooted in living tradition, as people seek direction and fidelity to the gospel in the modern world.

Most Catholic parishes have at least a dim shared sense of *what* they are about, individually and collectively, and *how* they are going about it. In these same parishes, a pervasive, pluralistic ignorance clouds *why* they exist. Indeed, most Catholic parishes haven't the slightest idea *why* they exist. Some individuals may feel they know why and would express their reasons with very strong conviction, but the parish as a whole lacks a shared sense of vision, unity of direction and purpose.

Chapter 5 described how virtually all human endeavors begin, grow and mature with a clear, shared sense of purpose. This legitimizes and necessitates being excited about communication, accountability, delegation of responsibility, authority and collegiality. There is no short-cut to structural reorganization, by-passing the rediscovery and excitement of discerning, articulating, proclaiming and affirming the vision (corporate challenge).

Pastoral Planning Cannot Be By-Passed

A parish first discerns, articulates, proclaims and receives affirmation for a corporate unifying vision which enfleshes where the parish *is* and where it *is called to be.* Having recalled the faith history of its people, the parish must evaluate and develop what it is doing individually and collectively, in the light of its parish vision. There is no great and universal pastoral plan to shape the ministry and missionary activity that a parish undertakes. This will depend upon the unique characteristics of the parish and its vision—the gap it's trying to close between where it is and where it is called to be.

Attitudes for Embracing Structural Changes

It is imperative to appreciate that structural change is only a matter of discovering *how* best to accomplish *what* needs to be done, in light of *why* a parish exists. Structures are not the purpose for which a parish exists, although some people think so. A particular structural alternative is certainly not more important. Structures or affection for a particular structural alternative is not fundamentally what we are about. Structures are an aid admittedly, a powerful force in helping or inhibiting activity faithful to our heritage and destiny. Structures are not ends in themselves. A structural alternative is not a god. Development of the best possible structure for effective communication, pastoral leadership, accountability and collegiality is a serious matter, but it is not an end in itself.

Structures and Levels of Presence

The optimum exercise of pastoral authority and subsidiarity is primarily a matter of *presence* between people with different responsibilities within a structure of differentiated *role authority.* Any structural alternative could and should be evaluated according to its capability for ensuring the higher levels of presence, along the continuum from symbolic presence to calling and being called. The best structure allows and promotes high levels of presence between servants and those being served.

The optimum experience of collegiality necessitates high levels of presence between and among those people *with the same role responsibility and authority* within the structure, thus ensuring maximum organizational integrity and vitality. In short, does the structure encourage communication among peers or groups of peers? Even more importantly, does the structure promote committed responding and the opportunity to call and be called by one another? This provides mutual support in their quest and also ensures effective collegiality which authors, empowers and invests in effective leadership.

Parish Climate and Structures

Any structural alternative could and should be evaluated on the basis of the organizational climate it encourages. Even a purposive parish will experience moments in which its predominant climate may be routine, supportive, task-directed or practical. It is difficult, if not impossible, and even unwise to try to sustain a purposive climate, day in and day out. However, any alternative parish structure can and should be evaluated on the basis of whether or not the structure intermittently encourages or even permits a purposive climate.

Readers of this material have, no doubt, enough experience in different parishes to recognize the following:

1. Structures and accompanying norms that never allow or promote any feeling or experience beyond the routine. These parishes sometimes almost seem to make a god of routinization.

2. Structures and norms which never allow or encourage anything beyond getting the job done.

3. Structures and norms which never allow or encourage anything but the experience of a warm, fuzzy community, where confrontation is avoided at all costs and the highest value is placed on individual comfort.

4. Structures and norms which never allow or encourage the growth and development of the persons involved in this essentially collective effort, beyond the infantilizing experience of an unhealthy dependence under a paternal and/or charismatic leader.

The Three Structural Alternatives

The difficulty, tensions and struggles surrounding the challenge to renew structures for communication, pastoral leadership, accountability, delegation of responsibility and collegiality involve the need to choose from among three structural alternatives: *trough, hierarchy* and *centrality.* The tension and conflict inherent in the choice involves the fundamental and often cloaked issue of the relationship between the exercise of pastoral authority and subsidiarity on the one hand and the experience of collegiality on the other. Do the two need to complement each other? Is there any relationship between these two principles of governance? If there is a relationship, what is its nature? Is it adversarial or complementary?

Is There a Case for Hierarchical Structures?

Some believe that Vatican I and Vatican II insist that the Church is hierarchical, with all revelation and therefore all authority coming from above and only through a hierarchy. For these people, collegiality has only a definite and specific meaning. They believe that collegiality has no generic value in relationship to authority beyond the specific relationship enunciated by Vatican II, that is, the complementarity between the authority of the Pope and the subsidiarity of bishops in relationship to collegiality within the college of bishops. They believe that beyond this level, where collegiality authors, empowers and guarantees leadership and vice versa, the principle of complementarity ends.

I frankly don't know what collegiality beyond this level means, if anything, to those who hold this position, presenting their case for the hierarchy. I think it must have no meaning at all, or simply means something that isn't supposed to exist or occur below the level addressed by Vatican II, in enunciating the relationship between the Pope and the college of bishops. The case for pure hierarchy obliterates the value or necessity for collegiality in the episcopate.

Those who put forth the case for hierarchical

structures in parishes often quote *Lumen Gentium* III, 18:

> The holders of office, who are invested with a sacred power, are in fact dedicated to promoting the interests of their brethren, so that all who belong to the people of God, and are consequently endowed with true Christian dignity, may, through their free and well-ordered efforts toward a common goal, attain to salvation.

> This Sacred Synod, following in the steps of the First Vatican Council, teaches and declares with it that Jesus Christ, the eternal pastor, set up the Holy Church by entrusting the apostles with their mission as he himself had been sent by the Father (cf. Jn. 20:21). He willed that their successors, namely the bishops, should be the shepherds in his Church until the end of the world. In order that the episcopate itself, however, might be one and undivided, he put Peter at the head of the other apostles, and in him he set up a lasting and visible source and foundation of the unity both of faith and communion. This teaching concerning the institution, the permanence, the nature and import of the sacred primacy of the Roman Pontiff and his infallible teaching office, the Sacred Synod proposes anew to be firmly believed by all the faithful, and, proceeding undeviatingly with this same undertaking, it proposes to proclaim publicly and enunciate clearly the doctrine concerning bishops, successors of the apostles, who together with Peter's successor, the Vicar of Christ and the visible head of the whole Church, direct the house of the living God.

The text which they quote does not mention hierarchical structures. It never calls the episcopate "the hierarchy." The principles pointed to in this text to define the case for a hierarchy are the principles emphasized in centrality.

In the text of the *Constitution on the Sacred Liturgy* (No. 42), the Council clearly and simply addresses the issue of pastoral authority:

> The pastor is the representative of the bishop of that flock which the bishop entrusts to his care. The pastor is the father of the local community. As ordained teachers and ministers of the word, priests (pastors) are placed in a position of considerable power, but it must be stressed that power is theirs in order that service might be better exercised. Authority *is* service. Where authority has not been acted upon in the context of "service," it has been experienced as either authoritarian or it has been abdicated out of a muddled sense of "democratic process."

This text, which makes no mention of collegiality, seems to presume it by describing authority as service. It does not address the issue of structure. It does not presume the necessity of hierarchical structures. In fact, it seems to warn against the deployment of hierarchical structures which discards the opportunity to experience authority as service and so make it authoritarian (unilateral, arbitrary and unaccountable). This text is also more compatible with the principles of centrality but it is often quoted to defend the case for hierarchy.

Is There a Case for Centrality Structures Which Guarantee Collegiality?
Cardinal Suenens in his book *Co-Responsibility in the Church* responds to the issue of pastoral authority as follows:

> . . .we must first rediscover the meaning of priestly collegiality. . . .No one is questioning the existence of a leader (pastor) as the one who is ultimately responsible. What is under discussion is the very nature of his function, and thus his role and place. The problem is not primarily one of safeguarding unity of command; it is much more profound than that. The fundamental role of the pastor is to make collegiality possible. He is its *guarantor.*

We can presume that Cardinal Suenens assumes a centrality model for the local church—diocese or parish.

The Heart of the Matter
Herein lies the difficulty of understanding the nature and meaning of the relationship between authority and subsidiarity on the one hand and collegiality on the other. What one presumes to be the best possible relationship between these two principles dictates one's bias in choosing between two structural alternatives—centrality and hierarchy.

In a centrality model the Pope presides in the center of the universal Church. He authors, empowers, and guarantees the collegiality of the bishops who, in turn, author and guarantee his leadership through their experience of collegiality. A bishop presides at the center of the diocese, authoring, empowering and guaranteeing the collegiality of pastoral leaders. Collegiality among pastoral leaders within a diocese invests in and guarantees the leadership of the bishop. (How this occurs most effectively will be written about at length in Volume III.) A pastor resides at the center of the parish, calling forth, authoring and empowering collegiality within the local church, which, in turn, undergirds his pastoral leadership (see Chapter 8).

In a hierarchical model, all authority belongs to the Pope, and since he can scarcely be expected to conduct the affairs of the local diocese, he bestows all authority on the person he chooses as the ordinary for that jurisdiction. All authority is bestowed by the ordinary on the pastor for a smaller jurisdiction.

In the hierarchical model one presumes that from the moment of commission, a Pope, bishop or pastor has one hundred percent of all of the authority ever needed to "pastor" effectively. The centrality model presumes that the moment of commission initiates pastoral leadership, the full meaning and exercise of pastoral authority being realized only when, through the process of collegiality, the pastor becomes the depositor of the hopes, dreams and aspirations—the vision of his people. Such authority is service incarnate.

The centrality model demands that structures of the local church should be faithful to the wisdom and spirit of Vatican II. Proponents of hierarchical structures point to the fact that Vatican II never concretely addressed the issue of complementarity between collegiality on the one hand and authority and subsidiarity on the other, except at the summit—between the Pope and the bishops. At the summit of a universal hierarchy, they should argue, the Church does not operate on a hierarchical model but reverences the principles inherent in a centrality model. However, they would insist that below the summit the Church must adopt hierarchical structures where collegiality is no longer viewed as complementary or even necessary. Some will go even further, saying that collegiality below the summit is adversative, hostile and a threat to the exercise of authority. Proponents of hierarchical structures maintain this position in spite of the fact that everything Vatican II teaches about authority at any level is absolutely contrary to the style of pastoral leadership *fostered* by hierarchical structures.

Is There a Case for Trough?

Vatican II created a thaw in the freeze on Church structures created by Vatican I. This thaw was so sudden that it caused a flood of questions and an avalanche of confusion and reactions. The council itself did not redefine authority in a way that would have clearly mandated replacing hierarchical structures with centrality structures at other levels besides the summit. Therefore, the vast majority of the Church could not appreciate the value of organizational integrity derived from complementarity between authority and collegiality.

What was heard instead most clearly and somewhat myopically from the Second Vatican Council was the call for more emphasis on co-responsibility and shared responsibility by those with a fresh preconciliar experience and memory of hierarchical authority as too authoritarian, unilateral and arbitrary. Thus, many parishes in today's Church went overboard to deinstitutionalize, to eradicate all structures, and quickly grasped for the image of community as an alternative to the monarchical structure of hierarchy.

In community, relationships were viewed as based solely on fraternal bonds. As such the exercise of authority was viewed as an obstacle to the experience of fraternity, collegiality and therefore the goal of community. This concept of community embraced a familial-type image in which relationships were founded only on mutual respect and love rather than on authority-subsidiarity roles and relationships. Community is the fullness of home, where we are known and loved, listened to and appreciated. Within the community there is equality whereby no one claims first place at the table when bread is broken together.

The exercise of authority and subsidiarity was presumed to be incompatible with the fulfillment of the aspiration for community. Authority was not viewed as authoring, empowering and guaranteeing collegiality, and therefore blocked fraternity and community. Authority and the exercise of its responsibility became a counter-sign to community. This shift of emphasis on community as pure collegiality without authority either signaled, reflected or supported the process of rethinking (and sinking) the parish into a structureless trough. With it came a multitude of abortive attempts to deinstitutionalize and declericalize the parish by allowing and even encouraging a certain amount of disorganization, now proven counterproductive to fulfilling the needs of people for ministering to one another and for mission to those beyond themselves.

Centrality Emphasizes Inter-Dependence Between Catholic People and Their Leaders

Centrality structures not only ensure the realization of the vision of Vatican II but they best achieve an effective relationship between the

Catholic people and their leadership for the on-going task of walking together with the Lord. The core problem in renewing parish structure is to effect an interdependent relationship between the Catholic people and their leadership. Quite frankly, I always cringe on the numerous occasions when I have been approached by a bishop, pastor, priest, lay person or religious announcing, "I have absolutely no faith or hope that the leadership of the Catholic Church will or can do anything to put vitality, life and excitement back in the Church. I put all my hope in the laity!"

I am embarrassed to say that I don't always respectfully disagree with the person at the time, but I do disagree with the comment. The Church will not rise like a sleeping giant, true to its heritage, to fulfill its great destiny, without its leadership. The Catholic people and their leadership, in my opinion, have to do it together or it won't be done at all.

Centrality Provides Common Ground for "Conservatives" and "Liberals"

In a centrality model, authority is always viewed as presiding "at the center" and not "on top of." In this model we presume the value and importance of both authority (and subsidiarity) and collegiality to fulfill and make possible the other. A centrality model not only allows us to escape the sad dilemma of feeling limited to a choice between the arbitrary, unilateral and unaccountable authority of a hierarchy versus the anarchy, disorganization and confusion of trough, but encourages us to see the vital organizational necessity for structures that guarantee complementarity between critically needed authoritative action and the collegiality which provides the forum for unity of purpose, direction, "common-union" and "common-unity."

Thus, the structures of a centrality model not only permit but guarantee communication and accountability in both directions. A centrality model is not merely a democratic process. Participative democracy would emphasize the flow of information to the center and de-emphasize the reverse process, thus making collegiality superior to authority, and would, no doubt, yield a congregationalism that would destroy the organizational integrity and vitality of the universal Church.

"Liberal" Catholicism is often associated with the value and importance placed on collegiality, while "conservative" Catholicism is associated with the exclusive emphasis on authority and subsidiarity. An understanding and appreciation of centrality should put an end to the bickering between people who like to believe that you can have one without the other. Maybe even conservatives and liberals within Catholicism will discover that they need each other!

Centrality Provides the Structures for Expanding Ministry

Organization is the key interface between individuals and society in mediating both stability and change. Societies rarely change individuals and individuals rarely change society. Rather the probabilities are that they will tend to invoke turmoil in each other. On the contrary, most social changes are mediated through organization and most individual changes occur within the context of an organization. If any effective impact is to be made in this world by the Catholic Church, it will have to be made within and through itself as an organization. Scattered individual vision and generosity are simply not enough. Nor can we be satisfied with only collegial community ties which are apt to yield an introverted community seeking to serve only itself, not thinking of its obligation to the neighborhood and the world.

A local parish experiences much tension as it struggles with the gospel imperative to be an apostolic organization dedicated to the well-being of all people. The task of becoming more apostolic is a task of reorganization and redefining roles and relationships. Parish structures need to change in order to allow not only the expression of ministerial priesthood but the priesthood of the faithful. As the concept of apostolic organization begins to shape, form and direct the parish in a new manner, the concept of ministries is not weakened but rather enhanced and enlarged. For it is not only the priests and professed religious who are called to minister, to serve, to engage in the works of redemption; it is the Catholic people. However, this extended and enlarged concept of ministry requires new and better structures, not merely fewer structures. In a very real way, laity are being called to participate *in the organization* of the Church. Thus, organization and structures are needed to allow and foster the ministry of the faithful.

The presumed incompatibility between authority and subsidiarity and collegiality, perpetuated by the assumption that the Church or local parish must develop a balance between hierarchy (institution) and community (trough), must yield to the concept of apostolic organization that includes all of the Catholic people. In a centrality model, both hierarchy (institution) and community (trough) give way to organizational structures that facilitate the complementarity of authority, subsidiarity and collegiality in which all the people of God participate.

Chapter Eight
The Construction and Functioning of a Centrality Model

Very often when staff hear, understand and gain an appreciation for the differences among parish structures that reflect and effect the three alternatives of centrality, hierarchy and trough, they soon begin asking questions about the functioning of a centrality model.

- How do you decide who should be on core staff?
- How do you select pastoral staff and persons in charge?
- What is the best rhythm for meetings of the core staff?
- What is the relationship of the core staff to the pastor and vice versa?
- How do you construct and design a centrality model for a particular parish?
- What is the difference between core staff and pastoral staff?
- What is the relationship between the clerical staff, which includes the pastor and all the priests ministering within the parish (sometimes including a resident and/or supply priest) and the other groups comprising the centrality structure?

In short, they begin asking questions about how a centrality model operates in the day-to-day life of a typical parish.

Principle of Span of Control

The construction of a parish structure for communication, accountability and pastoral leadership designed on a centrality model is created on the basis of only a few simple organizational principles. The first of these principles is that the span of control should not exceed five substantial relationships involving mutual accountability and support through the exercise of authority and subsidiarity. What does this mean concretely? Ideally speaking, it simply means that a core staff should not exceed five people with no more than twenty-five people on the pastoral staff, creating a five to one ratio of pastoral to core staff. Similarly, the number of persons-in-charge having direct access to a particular pastoral staff person should not exceed five. This principle should be honored in the structuring of relationships between people with fairly substantial responsibility. It is an important principle that should be honored in order to safeguard the quality of authority, ensure adequate support and effective supervision, and guarantee a vitality in the relationships between colleagues in a centrality structure. Pastors and individual parish staff are notorious for creating structures that offer ten, fifteen, twenty or even more people, with substantial responsibility, direct access to themselves. The violation of this principle in the name of generosity, availability and openness ultimately yields inadequate support, poor leadership and supervision, arbitrary and confused authoritative decisions and frustration for all involved. Limiting the span of control to five substantial relationships is based on a thoroughly researched theory of good organization.

Principle of Investing Responsibility

The second principle is that authority and responsibility should fundamentally and primarily be embodied in an individual. Concretely this principle argues against the desirability of selecting a married couple or any two persons to be in charge of a specific program, committee, parish organization or ministry team. Similarly it argues against the wisdom of co-pastorates and team pastorates. Furthermore it argues for clear lines of delegated responsibility and support, and therefore dictates the need to avoid sloppy structure, caused by disorganization, necessitating that the same person-in-charge receive support and be accountable to more than one pastoral staff person.

The Catholic Church has a two thousand year old tradition dictating that authority and responsibility are clearest when both are embodied in an individual. This tradition and the wisdom which undergirds it should not be taken lightly. For the most part, virtually all of the recent experiments of co-pastorates and team pastorates have failed for basically structural reasons and not because of personalities. Invariably in parishes where these experiments were tried, one of the individuals involved soon emerged as "the pastor."

The Principle of Divisional Integrity

The third principle involves the importance and value of divisional integrity in order to guarantee overall parish effectiveness of organizational structures. Thus, there should be some effort to obtain a structure that reflects the complementarity and integrity of all the various programs, organizations, ministry teams, etc., ministering under the auspices of any one member of the core staff. For example, a division would include all those things pertaining to marriage and family life. Similarly, the basis for divisional integrity could be worship and liturgy, or religious education and spiritual formation, or ministry, of care and discipleship, or mission, apostolic community and evangelization. These are just a few examples of primary thrusts upon which divisional integrity can be based. This principle should be honored in structuring the relationships between individual pastoral staff and persons-in-charge. Often the need to begin to achieve divisional integrity in the development of the centrality model requires that staff exchange responsibilities where working relationships have developed, and sometimes these exchanges require a real sacrifice. Of course, prudence and moderation dictate that it is not always possible to achieve abruptly all of the changes and exchanges of responsibility that a total honoring of this principle would require. The important thing is to begin. It makes no sense, on the other hand, to create a structural division with twenty-five to thirty different components that have almost no overlapping thrust or fundamental common denominator simply because these are all groups that have a current working relationship with a core staff member.

All Parishes—Large and Small—Need Structure

Virtually all Catholic parishes, large and small, have between fifty and one hundred and twenty-five components of their pastoral plan. None has less than fifty. Only a very few have more than one hundred. The average parish would have about seventy-five components. "Components" are the various programs, ministry teams, parish organizations, committees, etc. Individual ministry, although taken into account in the development of a parish's pastoral plan, is not made a part of the collective effort requiring communication and coordination among the various components of the collective, organized endeavor. Therefore, the typical centrality model honoring the principles mentioned above provides for a centrality structure of one pastor, a core staff of five or less (defining five or less primary divisions each having its own fundamental thrust and basis for divisional integrity), a pastoral staff of twenty-five or less persons, and one hundred and twenty-five or less persons-in-charge, each having his or her own specific area of responsibility and authority. Thus, the centrality model provides for two critically needed levels of "middle management" while it expands the avenues and opportunities available for ministry. The structure militates against the typical practice of relying on the same people for everything until they become exhausted, frustrated, annoyed and burned out.

Devising a Centrality Structure

Creating a centrality structure usually requires about two days of concerted effort by a core staff after they have completed their work on parish vision and have evaluated and developed their pastoral plan. Honoring the principles mentioned above, they usually begin by writing the name of each component of the pastoral plan on a 3 × 5 card, placing all of these cards in a large circle in a large working space. Their first task is to group these components according to the major divisions of pastoral thrust. Secondly, they look for obvious ways to group components within a primary division thrust that should be coordinated by a common pastoral staff person. Evaluating the overall structure and each division as they proceed, they decide, where possible, whom to ask to be the person-in-charge and to fill the various pastoral staff positions. Honoring the principle of span of control as much as possible, they decide when, if ever, the line of accessibility should be directly between the pastor and the person-in-charge or when this line of accessibility and communication would be better mediated by a core staff person or pastoral staff person or both.

CENTRALITY STRUCTURE

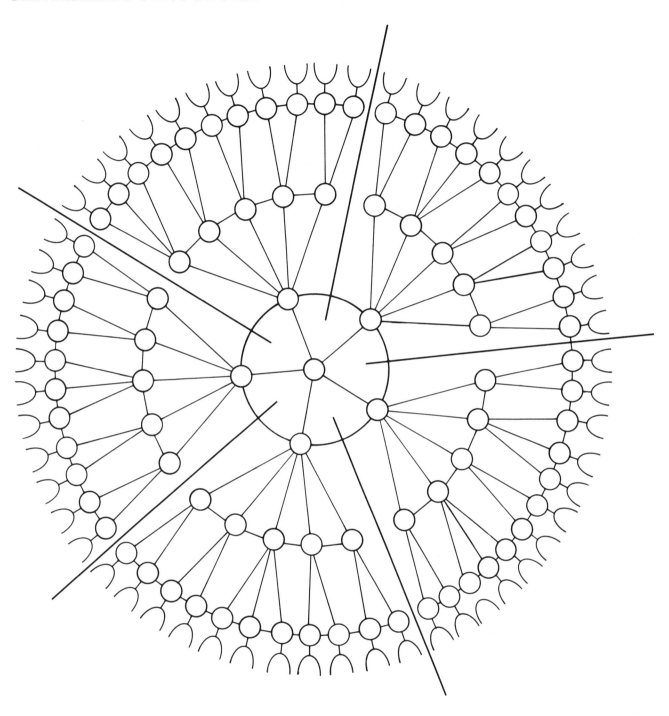

Pastor:
Core Staff: 2 to 5—establishes divisions
Pastoral Staff: 4 to 25—establishes Departments
Persons-In-Charge: up to 125—one for each program, ministry team, organization, etc.; actually the model can accommodate more than 125 components of a pastoral plan

Selection of Core Staff

Designing a centrality model for a particular parish and articulating the specific norms which will govern its operation initially is the responsibility of the core staff and the pastor. How is the core staff selected? There are no criteria which dictate who must be a part of the core staff because of their role and responsibility prior to the structural organization. All of the priests do not have to be on the core staff because they are ordained. There is no intrinsic necessity demanding that the school principal, the director of religious education, the youth minister, the permanent deacons or anyone else be invited to assume core staff responsibility. The principal criteria is simply: Whom does the pastor want on the core staff? With whom can he work best? Whom can he depend on, rely on and hold accountable? Who can work for him, and therefore make it easier for him to work with them? In whom does he place confidence? Whom does he perceive as sufficiently competent to achieve success? In my consultation I have seen priests, religious women and lay men and women achieve remarkable success as members of a core staff. Furthermore, I have experienced numerous occasions where it was obvious to everyone involved that it would be unwise and unjust to commission a particular priest, religious woman, school principal, permanent deacon or others with core staff authority and responsibility. There are, of course, other criteria but none close to the importance that must be placed on the pastor's preference or bias. No other criteria and no other person or persons can decide for the pastor, who should (or should not) be invited to be a part of the core staff. In selecting the core staff, a pastor should take into account not only his working relationship with each member of the core staff but the capacity of all to obtain a highly cohesive and productive, collective, working relationship.

The Pastor and the Core Staff's Collegiality

A fundamental responsibility of the pastor is to guarantee good collegiality among the core staff. Thus, the pastor authors, empowers and guarantees good task skills and presence, i.e., the quality of listening, understanding, responding, committed responding and fraternal calling among the members of the core staff. To ensure the pastor's capability to guarantee this collegiality, it is imperative that the pastor does not present himself or pretend to present himself as a colleague of the core staff or a participant in their collegiality. The colleagues of a pastor are other pastors. I must admit that I cringe on those occasions where I hear a pastor promising

to be a participant of the collegiality of the core staff. Such a promise not only means abdication; it condemns the core staff to flounder without the possibility of obtaining, experiencing or authoring collegiality, since this very promise withdraws the authority and support that makes collegiality possible. There is a significant difference between promising to participate in the collegiality versus promising to being committed to develop the collegiality of the core staff. In a centrality model, the pastor would be wise to make a commitment to obtain consensus among the core staff on decisions that affect the overall parish.

Core Staff's Collegiality and the Pastor's Authority

Members of the core staff have an individual and collective responsibility to work for and with the pastor to implement a unity of purpose, direction and action. Individually and collectively, members of the core staff should be committed to ensure and guarantee the effective exercise of the pastor's authority by being open to his call and yet willing, individually and collectively, to encourage, support, and criticize and challenge him. Members of the core staff, whether priest, religious woman or lay person, are first and foremost pastoral associates. They function in an associate capacity. While each member of the core staff will be responsible for an entire area of the total parish, the first, foremost and primary responsibility is to assist the pastor in working for common unity, common purpose, direction and action of the entire parish.

Factors Affecting Relationship Between Pastor and Core Staff

The relationship between the pastor and the core staff is, of course, vital. Therefore, it is important to examine some things that affect this relationship, reiterating specific norms that are generally effective for strengthening this relationship.

1. *Individual Meetings.* One issue that should be addressed is the matter of individual meetings for communication and supervision between the pastor and each member of the core staff. There is a strong tendency among pastors and many core staff people, too, to assume that regularly scheduled meetings of the pastor with the entire core staff eliminate the necessity for the pastor to meet individually, on a regular basis, with each member of the core staff. Most pastors would like to operate on this assumption because they don't like to supervise and because they somehow manage to convince themselves that regularly scheduled individual

meetings symbolize a lack of trust in the competence and integrity of a core staff member. Consistently, we have found that the omission of these individual meetings for communication, accountability and supervision has three predictably negative effects. First, the quality of the meetings of the pastor and the entire core staff becomes more boring and frustrating because much of the time at these gatherings is wasted when the pastor takes turns discussing issues with members of the core staff that are of no concern to the others. Second, because individual meetings for communication, accountability and supervision have been eliminated the associate member of the core staff soon begins to experience that he or she is less able to speak in the name of the pastor or exercise effective pastoral prerogatives with regard to the problems or issues being addressed in that area of parish functioning for which he or she is responsible. Finally, the elimination of these individual sessions for supervision, accountability and communication begins to undermine the confidence and trust of the pastor in each member of the core staff, because without these meetings each member of the core staff can't possibly know the pastor's heart and therefore represent him and speak in his name, addressing the issues and problems of their areas. Thus, while collective meetings of the core staff with the pastor are imperative to ensure their individual and collective responsibility for the unity of the parish, individual meetings for supervision, communication and accountability are equally imperative to guarantee the respective capability of each member of the core staff, to provide optimum leadership in the area of parish functioning for which each is responsible.

2. *"Leap-Frog Maneuvers."* Another issue affecting the vitality of the relationship between pastor and core staff involves the matter of "leap-frog maneuvers". It is inevitable that numerous occasions will occur in which persons-in-charge, pastoral staff, program staff, members of a ministry team and others will demand and expect direct accessibility to the pastor on issues causing them concern. They will expect and demand this direct access, often very early, even knowing that their expectation and demand violates and undermines the very structure that ensures effective authority, mutual accountability and collegiality. Both the core staff and the pastor are responsible for ensuring the vitality of this structure. Particularly, the pastor should realize the power and responsibility bestowed upon him for minimizing and discouraging "leap-frog maneuvers" by pastoral staff, persons-in-charge and others.

The pastor can discourage and minimize such activity by discouraging and even disallowing confidential and privileged communication between himself and others seeking to violate the structure that ensures organizational integrity and effective authority. The pastor can and should use such occasions to invite and challenge people to utilize the centrality structure by taking their concern to the person most immediately and directly able to respond decisively. The pastor can, of course, invite them to bring their concerns to him later if they are not satisfied with the handling of the matter on a more peripheral level. Even then, however, he should promise to fully seek the perspective, advice and counsel of those delegated with authority and responsibility regarding this matter. This is a difficult adjustment for most pastors who want to be "nice guys" and who, being human, are flattered when they are approached to settle a matter or resolve a conflict by making a decision. However, if a pastor (or core staff member, for that matter) repeatedly violates the structure for ensuring effective leadership, mutual accountability and communication, he or she ultimately destroys the foundation for organizational integrity, effective leadership, mutual accountability and unity of purpose and action. Soon anything, everything, anyone and everyone has direct accessibility to the pastor, absolutely guaranteeing that the exercise of pastoral authority will soon become unilateral, arbitrary, authoritarian and ineffectual.

3. *The Pastor as Minister.* Another issue effecting the vitality of the relationship between pastor and core staff involves an appreciation of the fact that besides being a minister to ministers, the pastor is also a minister. The pastor is the primary supervisor of the parish, ensuring that all other ministry and ministers have the effective support, accountability and benefit of colleagues to which they are entitled. However, the pastor is also a priestly minister who should know what part of his own ministry is most essential to himself. This ministry certainly varies and is different among pastors. This essential part of his ministry is something a pastor may certainly share, but he will not—indeed, he cannot—completely delegate it to others without feeling terribly diminished as a minister. Therefore, it is wise that a pastor and core staff recognize the need and provide effective opportunities for the pastor to utilize fully the gifts which are a part of this ministry. Very frequently this means utilizing opportunities to call on the pastor as a resource for programs, ministry teams, organizations, etc., operating under the auspices of a core staff member. The demands for

priestly ministry, pastoral supervision and pastoral administration will prohibit the pastor from directly taking charge of ministry teams, programs or organizations except in a few parishes where other priests are willing and happy to take much more than their share of the priestly ministries. It is imperative that a pastor and core staff appreciate the direct ministerial-giftedness of the pastor and utilize it to the benefit of the parish and the well-being of the pastor.

Summary of Norms Affecting Pastor and Core Staff Relationship

The following are norms which, generally speaking, guarantee productive and vital relationship between the pastor and the core staff.

1. The pastor is the convenor and guarantor of effective collegiality among members of the core staff. He is committed to obtaining a consensus among the core staff on decisions that affect the total parish.

2. The core staff individually and collectively are committed to support and challenge the pastor, thus guaranteeing his effectiveness as pastor and the most effective exercise of his authority and prerogatives.

3. Core staff function with the pastor and for the pastor in an associate capacity whether priest, religious or lay person. The pastor and each member of the core staff are responsible for establishing a regular rhythm of meeting individually for supervision, problem solving, communication and accountability.

4. Individual core staff persons provide the day-to-day pastoral presence and authority in the area of the total parish where each has pastoral responsibility. The pastor's presence at what occurs in areas such as programs, staff meetings, etc., and his role at such gatherings should be determined mutually, as much as possible, by the pastor and the core staff person responsible for that area.

5. The pastor and the core staff are committed to utilize the structure for effective communication, accountability and the exercise of pastoral authority by encouraging that decisions be made and problems solved by the person with responsibility closest to the issue. All will discourage "leap-frog maneuvers" utilizing attempts to violate the structure as an opportunity to reinforce and strengthen its value and importance.

The Core Staff's Collective Relationship

The collective relationship among those who comprise the core staff is as important as their individual and collective relationship to the pastor. All members of the core staff should be committed to reverence, respect and utilize their different gifts, talents and strengths. Furthermore, they need to commit themselves to develop their presence to a level at which they are intimate enough to be comfortable with responding to each other candidly, able to challenge one another, call each other forth and help shape each other's role and responsibilities. They should pray together, share faith experiences, and examine and develop their collective spirituality, thus ensuring a spiritual foundation for their individual and collective leadership.

The core staff should make a commitment to one another to make creative use of the tensions and conflicts that arise, engaging these moments as an opportunity for learning rather than an obstruction. As individuals, each provides the day-to-day pastoral presence for a substantial area of the total parish. However, since their primary responsibility is for the total parish, they should know, understand and appreciate the peculiar challenges of their respective divisional responsibility well enough virtually to be prepared to take one another's place if necessary. Core staff are generalists in appreciation of their primary role. Therefore, it is not absurd to presume that they could be interchangeable.

Summary of Norms Affecting the Core Staff

In summary, the following norms, generally speaking, guarantee an effective and productive relationship between and among members of the core staff.

1. Each member of the core staff is committed to reverence and respect the different gifts among them but also challenge one another mutually and interdependently helping to shape their respective roles and responsibilities.

2. The core staff is committed to pray together, share faith experiences and reflect together spiritually to ensure the spiritual support and the spiritual foundations for their individual and collective leadership.

3. The core staff is committed to make creative use of the tensions and conflicts that arise between them and to sharpen and to confront differences of opinion as an opportunity to improve their individual and collective leadership. The inevitability of these tensions, conflicts and differences should not be viewed as an obstruction.

4. Core staff shall assist in mutually and interdependently clarifying and determining one another's role.

Core Staff Responsibility for Ministry, Mission and Renewal

The core staff, with individual and collective associate authority, together with the pastor, have the most central responsibility for the overall parish, its vision, its pastoral plan and the vitality of its structure for effective authority, communication and accountability. In communication with the entire parish, and mutually accountable to the total parish, made possible by the centrality model, they are responsible with the pastor for the inward ministerial thrust of the parish and its outward mission. The core staff are responsible for the on-going renewal of the parish. Each core staff person provides the day-to-day pastoral presence and authority for the area of the parish for which he or she is responsible. In a very real way, each core staff person must become for the pastoral staff and persons-in-charge within his or her division what the pastor is for the core staff. Individually each must see the coordination and integration of the various ministry teams, programs and organizations within the respective divisions. Each must be open to listen, to lead, to challenge and be challenged by the pastoral staff and persons-in-charge of ministering and missionary activity within his or her area of responsibility. Each member of the core staff authors, empowers and guarantees effective leadership and effective collegiality for his or her respective area.

Usually the core staff is the only collective group that has a corporate or collective responsibility to the pastor. All other groups, comprising the staff of a program, the ministers of a ministry team or the members of an organization, will typically experience their collegiality authored, empowered and guaranteed by a leader within the centrality structure other than the pastor, i.e., core staff, pastoral staff or person-in-charge.

The pastor and the core staff, who are ultimately accountable for fostering the "common-unity" of the total parish, are also ultimately accountable to empower parish leaders to ensure the vitality of every component of the parish's ministry and mission. Therefore, it is their responsibility to provide laity with access to participate in the overall ministry and mission of the parish by selecting, training, authorizing and resourcing (S.T.A.R.). The pastoral staff and persons-in-charge provide the critically needed "middle management," thus providing more laity with the opportunity to minister.

Meetings of Core Staff

Of course, the core staff cannot deliver what is expected, fulfilling their responsibility, without meeting. How frequently should a core staff meet? How much time for meeting as a core staff is enough? How much time is too much? When is the best time to meet? What is the best rhythm and procedure for organizing such a meeting?

Many different kinds of formats have been tried and experimented with: as a result, I have come to the opinion that core staff really need to formulate a rhythm of two different kinds of regularly scheduled meetings—weekly meetings and profound issue gatherings.

Weekly Meetings

The first of these gatherings is a weekly meeting of the core staff and the pastor scheduled for an hour and a half to two hours at the most. It has not proved feasible or adequate to schedule these "business meetings" either bi-weekly or bi-monthly. Ideally, the best possible time for these short meetings is Monday morning after the last morning Mass, yet early enough to schedule a Monday morning funeral. This, of course, means that if a funeral occurs on a Monday morning, it would be scheduled for approximately 11:00 A.M. Monday morning is ideal because it occurs early enough in the week so that decisions can still be printed in the bulletin. Also, the Monday morning meeting provides ample time to follow up on any decisions that may affect the approaching weekend liturgy. Midweek and weekend meetings invariably seem to occur too late to act on the decisions reached. Afternoon and early evening meetings usually find everyone exhausted. Late evening or weekend meetings usually have to compete with a multitude of other gatherings requiring the presence of the pastor and the core staff. The most feasible time to regularly schedule the weekly meeting will vary from parish to parish and of course will be influenced by the schedules of lay men and women on the core staff. The important thing is that they are scheduled regularly. These meetings should begin and end promptly. About one-third to one-half of the time should be devoted to scriptural reflection, prayer and sharing faith experiences. The remaining time should be utilized to quickly assemble the agenda, requiring information sharing, discussion and decision, avoiding any discussion or deliberation until it has been preliminarily decided what to handle in the time available and how much time to allocate to each item. Formulating the agenda should take no more than ten minutes, after which the business meeting begins, covering each item as planned, with someone responsible to chair the meeting and someone else responsible for the basic recording of the agenda and the decisions reached.

Although many procedures for formulating the agenda prior to the weekly meeting have been attempted, none has proven successful.

Profound Issue Gatherings

A second kind of regularly scheduled meeting is needed to handle different kinds of problems and issues from those addressed in the weekly meetings. In short, a pastor and core staff need to address what I have come to term by way of analogy both "one-ten issues" and "two-twenty issues." The "one-ten issues" consist of problems and items that require very little to modest amounts of discussion. "Two-twenty issues" are much larger issues which require considerable discussion, weighing alternatives, etc. I use the analogy to one-ten and two-twenty current to make the point that you can't "run" a 220 appliance on 110 current no matter how many times you plug it in. Similarly, a pastor and core staff cannot do justice to "220 issues" by addressing these problems in a single or even consecutive weekly business meetings. A pastor and core staff should formulate a regularly scheduled rhythm for meeting together to face into these larger issues. The best, most effective rhythm for the second kind of gathering is to set aside one full day every month or two full days every two months.

Summary of Norms Affecting Core Staff Responsibility for Parish

The following norms, generally speaking, guarantee an effective and productive performance of the core staff's responsibility to the parish.

1. The core staff shall meet regularly on a weekly and a monthly (or bi-monthly) basis to work with the pastor to foster unity of purpose, direction and action in helping to shape parish ministry and mission.

2. The core staff, as associates of the pastor, collectively work for the pastor to ensure integrity of parish vision, pastoral plan and parish structure.

3. Core staff, working for and with the pastor, are responsible for the on-going renewal of the parish, seeing to it that this renewal is grounded in the faith experiences of the parishioners.

4. Each member of the core staff provides "pastoral presence" and represents the collective authority of the core staff for that area of the total parish for which he or she is responsible.

5. The core staff is responsible and accountable to listen and respond to parishioners through their working relationship with the pastoral staff, persons-in-charge, those ministering in the various components of the pastoral plan and all parishioners who are the recipients, participants and benefactors of parish ministry and mission.

6. The core staff is responsible to empower people to participate in the ministry and mission of the parish, i.e. to S.T.A.R. (select, train, authorize and resource) laity and others as pastoral staff and persons-in-charge (leaders and ministers).

7. The primary responsibility and greatest priority of each member of the core staff is to the total parish and the unity of the parish. The second priority and second responsibility of each member of the core staff is to his or her unique and special area of responsibility within the total parish.

8. The core staff are responsible for ensuring the coordination and complementarity among the major areas (divisions) of parish mission and ministry.

9. The core staff shall meet regularly to coordinate the primary divisions, offering one another encouragement, support, criticism, challenge and performance evaluation.

10. The core staff is responsible for challenging the parish as a whole and the various organizations, programs and ministry teams around spiritual growth and clarity of purpose and action.

11. Core staff work for and with the pastor in an associate capacity (whether priest, religious or lay person) to ensure the "common-unity" (community) and "common-union" (communion) for the planning and implementation of the parish vision, pastoral plan and centrality structure.

12. The core staff, with the pastor, are responsible for guaranteeing that the exercise of authority and subsidiarity complements, authors, empowers and guarantees collegiality and vice versa within the centrality structure.

Relationship Between Core Staff and Priest Staff

Before discussing the next level of responsibility within the centrality model, "pastoral staff," it would be wise to make a few comments about the relationship between core staff and priest staff. Do priests ever need to meet alone apart from the core staff? Does the introduction of a core staff abdicate or eradicate the possibility, advisability, feasibility and desirability for collective priestly leadership, since the core staff is oftentimes comprised of non-ordained as well as ordained persons?

Priestly Leadership

My previous experience overwhelmingly points to the desirability to reverence the necessity for integral, collective, priestly leadership. Whether all of the priests are on the core staff or not, it is imperative that the priests ministering within a parish, meet frequently enough to ensure collective thrust in three fundamental areas that are essential to parish, priestly ministry.

1. *Teaching Function.* The first of these is the teaching function of priesthood. Individually and collectively, priestly presence brings to the assembly of parishioners an awareness and appreciation that all, through baptism, are privileged to share the common bond of sonship and daughtership in God. The ordinary response of parishioners to this collective priestly leadership will be ministry, both individual and communal, by all the members for the welfare of the rest of the community and for those with whom the community interacts. Apart from the core staff, priests should reflect together on Jesus' spirit and actions alive in the collective efforts of the parish to touch the critical centers and sources of destruction of human life, thus guaranteeing collective priestly wisdom in the midst of this struggle.

2. *Cultic Function.* The second fundamental role of priestly ministry involves cultic function. Through the sacraments, and especially the weekly eucharistic liturgy, the priests lead the assembly in the celebration of its shared life in the Lord. These liturgies call to mind the joys and sorrows of the week past and look forward to the challenges confronting the parish. Liturgy has the power of touching people at key points in their lives. Therefore, collective priestly leadership is needed in tense moments of joy, pain, human passages and conflicts to point out God's presence and to ensure the solidarity and mutual love and respect among the parishioners.

3. *Prophetic Function.* The third fundamental role of priestly ministry involves prophetic function. Collectively, the leadership of priests takes on the new dimension of rabbi, the prophets who stand with their people in special moments of joy and sorrow, peace and tension, helping them to make sense of the events surrounding them in the light of the Sacred Scripture. While the priests must always be responsible to the local needs and aspirations of the parish, they cannot abdicate their responsibility to preside at the interface of the parish with the diocese, and with the universal Church of which the parish is only a part. Thus, collectively, the priest's function is as "authenticator" of the community's faith, discernment and action, ensuring that the parish remains faithful to the history, traditions and wider dimensions of the universal Church.

The Need for Priest Meetings

Individually, the priestly resources of the parish cannot even begin to fulfill their teaching, cultic and prophetic functions. If the priests of a parish are going to provide any effective priestly leadership with respect to any of these three functions, they must meet intermittently to ensure and guarantee a collective priestly thrust in all three areas. Their collective effort to ensure priestly unity in their teaching, cultic and prophetic function will strengthen the effectiveness of the core staff. Where attempts to ensure collective, priestly leadership are omitted, core staffs find it much more difficult to function effectively. Yet, it consistently occurs that priests are reluctant and hesitant to meet regularly for fear that by so doing they will undermine the authority and responsibility of the core staff. In fact, the opposite is true.

The Pastoral Staff Role

Whereas the core staff is fundamentally and primarily responsible for the "common-unity" (community) and "common-union" (communion), unity of purpose, direction and action for the total parish, and, secondarily, responsible for their respective area (division), the priority of these two functions is reversed for the pastoral staff. A pastoral staff person is primarily responsible for coordinating, usually through persons-in-charge, a "department" comprised of approximately five or less different parish organizations, ministry teams or programs having some common denominator. For example, one pastoral staff person may coordinate two, three, four or five different components of the overall pastoral plan that addresses marriage and family life. Another may be coordinating different components of ministry of care or liturgy, etc. Core staff people are responsible for divisions. Pastoral staff people coordinate different programs, ministry teams and organizations within a division.

Pastoral Staff—Coordinators

Working for and with the core staff person to whom they are mutually accountable, pastoral staff author, empower and guarantee collegiality among the persons-in-charge of the various components of the pastoral plan which each is responsible for coordinating. Thus, pastoral staff persons are primarily coordinators and *not implementers* of responsibilities delegated to the persons-in-charge of various components of the pastoral plan.

Meetings of Core Staff and Pastoral Staff

In most parishes the core staff will find it desirable to gather together all pastoral staff for intermittent meetings. Some collegiality and mutual support should be experienced among the entire pastoral staff. However, since this is usually a fairly large group of approximately twenty-five people, meetings of the total pastoral staff are usually infrequent and primarily for the purpose of sharing information. Collegiality of pastoral staff is better guaranteed by more frequent and/or in-depth meetings of pastoral staff within a division.

Meetings of Pastoral Staff within a Division

Whereas meetings of the entire pastoral staff with the core staff will occur once a month or once every two months for no more than two hours, meetings of pastoral staff within one of the major divisions will occur as frequently as is deemed necessary by the core staff person responsible for the division. These pastoral staff meetings, by division, usually occur once every two weeks and sometimes weekly for the duration of about two hours.

Relationship of Total Pastoral Staff to Core Staff

The total pastoral staff has a collective corporate relationship with the total core staff. They do not have a collective relationship with the pastor. Pastoral staff within the major divisions have a collective relationship with the core staff person responsible for that division. He or she authors, empowers and guarantees the collegiality of pastoral staff within that division, and they in turn are responsible for authoring, empowering and guaranteeing the effective pastoral authority of the core staff person.

The core staff person-in-charge of a particular division should establish a regular rhythm of meeting individually with each pastoral staff person in his or her division for supervision, mutual problem solving, communication and accountability. These individual meetings of core staff with each of the pastoral staff within their division are desirable for the same reasons that the pastor should establish a regular rhythm of individual meetings with his respective core staff members.

Interchangeability of Pastoral Staff

Pastoral staff members are *not* easily interchangeable with regard to their respective responsibilities as are core staff. I emphasized earlier that core staff should help to shape one another's role and know one another's divisional responsibilities

well enough to be virtually prepared to exchange roles and responsibilities. While this is true for core staff whose primary responsibility is to foster total parish unity, it is not true for pastoral staff whose primary responsibility is the coordination of specific programs, ministry teams and organizations with a common denominator and, therefore, a common link through the presence of a pastoral staff member. Pastoral staff members are *not* easily interchangeable as are core staff because they are selected, trained and authorized to coordinate persons-in-charge of efforts that require the gift of specific knowledge, attitude and skills. Pastoral staff members, of course, need also to share the particular gifts of the persons-in-charge whom they are coordinating. Pastoral staff are not selected, trained and authorized to coordinate specific components of a pastoral plan merely because they are excellent coordinators. They have to be gifted as coordinators, but they must also have specific knowledge, attitudes and skills appropriate for the departments they are coordinating. In short, these requirements make them much less interchangeable in comparison to the members of the core staff.

Pastoral Staff Functions

Each individual pastoral staff member provides the primary, emotional, pastoral and spiritual support for the persons-in-charge whose efforts they coordinate. The pastoral staff member authors, empowers and guarantees the collegiality among those persons-in-charge, who in turn invest in and support his or her authority. Thus, a pastoral staff member should intermittently gather together the persons-in-charge of efforts he or she is coordinating, for sharing prayer and faith experiences, mutual problem-solving, support and challenge. It is imperative that individual pastoral staff members meet regularly on an individual basis with the persons-in-charge, in charge of organizations, ministry teams and programs coordinated by them, to provide supervision and counsel as required and to help make decisions and implement the activities within each component of the pastoral plan.

Summary of Norms Affecting Pastoral Staff

Pastoral staff are the primary coordinators of the pastoral plan in a centrality model. Within the structure for communication, accountability, collegiality and the exercise of effective authority, they primarily fulfill the "middle management" responsibility. Their role, responsibility and function is critical because they provide the critically needed "middle management" which is absolutely necessary to expand the number of people involved in ministry and pastoral leadership. The following norms, generally speaking, guarantee an effective and productive performance of the pastoral staff responsibility to the parish.

1. Individually and collectively, pastoral staff are primarily responsible for coordinating approximately five or fewer different parish organizations, ministry teams or programs. Their secondary responsibility is to foster "common-unity" (community) and "common-union" (communion), unity of purpose, direction and action for the total parish. Thus, the priorities of two essential functions, coordination versus fostering total parish unity, are exactly the opposite of these two functions of core staff.

2. Individual pastoral staff author, empower and guarantee collegiality among approximately five or fewer persons-in-charge who in turn invest in and support the authority of the pastoral staff member.

3. Pastoral staff members are primarily coordinators and *not implementers* of responsibilities delegated to persons-in-charge of various components of the pastoral plan.

4. Collegiality of pastoral staff is best guaranteed by intermittent meetings of pastoral staff within a division. Occasional meetings primarily for the purpose of sharing information may occur involving the total pastoral staff.

5. Total pastoral staff have a collective and corporate relationship with the total core staff. They do not have a corporate relationship with the pastor.

6. The core staff person with responsibility for a particular division should establish a regular rhythm of meeting individually with each pastoral staff member in his or her division for supervision, mutual problem-solving, communication and accountability.

7. Pastoral staff should be selected, trained and authorized to coordinate specific components of the pastoral plan on the basis of their ability to coordinate the specific knowledge, attitudes and skills appropriate for the "department" he or she is coordinating.

8. Individual pastoral staff provide the primary emotional, pastoral, spiritual and supervisory support for the persons-in-charge whose efforts they coordinate. Thus, each individual pastoral staff member should establish a regular rhythm of meeting individually and collectively with the person-in-charge of various components of the pastoral plan comprising their "department."

Responsibility of Persons-In-Charge

Persons-in-charge are those responsible and accountable for providing leadership and supervision within a specific component of the pastoral plan. As mentioned earlier, the centrality model provides a structure that will accommodate approximately one hundred and twenty-five different persons-in-charge. Each person-in-charge is responsible and accountable for the quality of relationships and the planning and implementation of activities within his or her respective organization, program or ministry team.

Each person-in-charge is responsible and accountable for authoring, empowering and guaranteeing the collegiality of the people (ministers) who comprise a particular organization, program or ministry team. This collegiality in turn authors, empowers and guarantees the effective exercise of authority of the persons-in-charge. Therefore, each person-in-charge is responsible for establishing a regular rhythm of meeting for prayer, sharing faith experiences, planning and decision-making among the membership of the organization, program or ministry team for which he or she is responsible. Each person-in-charge helps to foster the unity of direction and purpose of the total parish by helping to direct the activities of his or her respective organization, program or ministry team in concert with the overall vision and pastoral plan of the total parish.

Fostering Collegiality among Persons-In-Charge

The primary source of collegiality among persons-in-charge will be the intermittent meetings scheduled by the pastoral staff member who coordinates the overlapping efforts of approximately five or fewer different organizations, programs or ministry teams. Secondary collegial support for persons-in-charge will be obtained and experienced by occasional intermittent gatherings of all the persons-in-charge constituting a particular division. These latter meetings would, of course, be called by the core staff person responsible for a particular division, and he or she would, no doubt, plan and execute these gatherings with the aid and participation of the pastoral staff with that division. Feasibly, very little can be done to promote collegiality among all those persons-in-charge within the parish since there are so many. However, it is possible and desirable to call a "leadership conference" approximately once a year. The invitation to attend these conferences should be extended, of course, to all pastoral staff and persons-in-charge, thus necessitating a design for exchanging ideas and sharing information and hopes, dreams and aspirations among approximately one hundred and fifty-six people—one hundred and twenty-five persons-in-charge, twenty-five pastoral staff, five core staff and one pastor.

Summary of Norms Affecting Persons-In-Charge

The following norms, generally speaking, guarantee an effective and productive performance on the part of the persons-in-charge of the different organizations, programs and ministry teams comprising the overall pastoral plan of the parish.

1. Persons-in-charge are those responsible and accountable for providing leadership and supervision for a specific parish organization, program or ministry team.

2. Each person-in-charge is responsible and accountable for authoring, empowering and guaranteeing the collegiality of the people (ministers) who comprise the membership of a particular program, organization or ministry team. This collegiality in turn undergirds and helps to author, empower and guarantee the authority of the persons-in-charge.

3. Pastoral staff are responsible for establishing a regular rhythm for meeting individually and collectively with the persons-in-charge of their respective "departments." The individual meetings ensure adequate support, supervision and accountability. The collective meetings provide collegial support for persons-in-charge, thus helping to author, empower and guarantee the authority of individual pastoral staff.

4. Each person-in-charge is responsible and accountable for the quality of relationships and the planning and implementation of activities within his or her respective organization, program or ministry team.

5. Very little can be done to accomplish collegiality among all the persons-in-charge with the exception of an annual or occasional "leadership conference."

6. Persons-in-charge should direct, supervise and lead the activities of their respective organization, program or ministry team so that its effort is in concert with the overall vision and pastoral plan of the total parish.

7. Persons-in-charge should be selected on the basis of their ability to lead a particular organization, program or ministry team, thus pointing to the desirability of both general leadership skills and specific knowledge, skills, and attitudes necessary to lead a particular component of the overall pastoral plan.

Concluding Remarks

The advice given so far should be weighed and taken simply as advice. It includes criteria that have typically proven well worth considering in the selection of core staff, pastoral staff and persons-in-charge. The advice contains norms which, generally speaking, guarantee a productive and effective core staff, pastoral staff and persons-in-charge component of a centrality model. However, these criteria, these norms and this advice must be weighed and considered with other criteria in the construction and design of a centrality model for a particular parish.

In this description I have attempted to present a clear picture of how a centrality model operates in the day-to-day life of a typical parish. I have deliberately emphasized what has generally proven to be most effective for establishing a regular rhythm of meetings that will ensure that authority fulfills its obligation to author, empower and guarantee collegiality, showing in turn how this collegiality undergirds, supports, authors, empowers and guarantees the effective exercise of authority within the entire centrality structure.

I am sure that pastors and parish staffs, hearing this description of a centrality model for the first time, will invariably feel overwhelmed by the prospect and challenge for creating a structure for pastoral leadership that includes a core staff of approximately five people, a pastoral staff of approximately twenty-five people and approximately one hundred and twenty-five persons-in-charge. This centrality model, and the structure through which it operates, is a whole new structure for communication, accountability, collegiality and the exercise of pastoral authority which is extremely difficult to picture as taking the place of existing structures or lack of structures. Such structural change, while scary and difficult to accomplish at first, is potentially the most powerful kind of renewal for providing laity with more access to ministry and pastoral leadership and guaranteeing the critically needed "middle management" that expanding the kinds of ministries and the number of people involved in ministry requires.

At the risk of sounding slightly pompous, there is absolutely no doubt in my mind that the Catholic parish will continue to experience a tremendous escalation in terms of the kinds of ministries parishioners want, need and expect. In short, we are a people who want and need more and more varied ministry. There is absolutely no sign that people will be satisfied with a minimum of programs, a few basic organizations and the limited ministry that can be provided by the precious few ordained and non-ordained paid staff of the parish.

The centrality model provides a structure that allows the parish to accommodate escalating diversity of ministries without burning out the same people. This expansion and accommodation can be accomplished within a centrality model, appreciating both the need for overall organizational integrity and the necessity for complementarity between the principles of collegiality and authority. Although it is overwhelming to face the challenge of creating a centrality model, the alternatives are certainly less desirable. One alternative would be to introduce hierarchical structures which will violate complementarity between the principles of collegiality and authority and ultimately collapse into the structuralist trough for the previously explained reasons. Another alternative is to avoid the challenge of establishing any structure for communication, accountability and the exercise of pastoral authority. Such a choice will deeply frustrate and violate parishioners by depriving everyone of the diversity of ministry desired and deserved. At the same time, this choice will quickly burn out the staff and those few dedicated parishioners trying to fill a void and achieve overall organizational integrity.

Therefore, as overwhelming and as difficult as it may first seem to embrace and face the challenge of creating an effective centrality model, there is no other alternative, presuming we maintain that there is a value in having large parishes. Failing to embrace and face into this challenge, everyone, parishioners and staff alike, will yearn for small "manageable" parishes.

Chapter Nine
A Parish Council and the Centrality Model

The spirit of collegiality fostered by the Second Vatican Council has resulted in the development of parish councils in most parishes in the United States and throughout the world. The concept of parish councils is relatively new, however, and the experience of shared responsibility in the Church today is still a learning process. Unfortunately, much confusion exists about the nature of the local parish. This confusion spills over and presents an obstacle to the involvement and participation of lay men and women in the ministry and mission of the parish. Diocesan officials, pastors, parish staffs and laity are usually very quickly excited and enthusiastic about the concepts and prospects of a centrality model for communication, accountability, authority and collegiality. However, not infrequently they immediately ask, "What does this mean for the parish council?" "What is the role of the parish council in such a model?" "How can a parish council fit within a centrality structure?"

Functions of Parish Councils
Examination of parish council guidelines written by several different dioceses and the reading of many, many parish constitutions drafted by parish councils to formulate guidelines for their own function reveal that, generally speaking, there are seven articulated or implied functions that most parish councils undertake:

1. Policy making, decision-making and priority setting.
2. Think-tank, advisory board and brain-trust.
3. Implementers of specific ministries and programs.
4. Evaluators of the overall parish and various programs from the perspective of the "person in the pew."

5. Intensive forum to ensure complementarity between "ordained and non-ordained staff" and the "priesthood of the laity."
6. Creators and implementers of their own programs.
7. Long-range planning and the development of parish-community relations.

Specific parish councils, of course, may emphasize one or two of these functions, and the functions receiving greatest emphasis vary among councils, but, by and large, all councils appear to embrace all seven functions to some degree. Before examining the alternatives for integrating a parish council with the centrality model, emphasizing these different functions, it would be worthwhile to review, first of all, how and why parish councils came into being.

Genesis of Parish Councils
Recalling the evolution of parish structures from centrality to hierarchy and, finally, trough, virtually all parish councils and the concept of parish council were born during that period in which everybody was experiencing the breakdown and disintegration of hierarchical structures, giving birth to anarchy and the unstructured condition of the trough. The mood and the climate of the time were clear. People were tired and frustrated with the unilateral, arbitrary and unaccountable exercise of authority by those who saw their position as "on top" rather than "in the center" of an essentially collective endeavor. Laity felt infantilized, resentful and sometimes incensed by analogies drawn from Scripture that compared them to sheep or children. The hierarchical structure clearly disenfranchised laity from having a mature and adult voice, participation or responsibility within a parish.

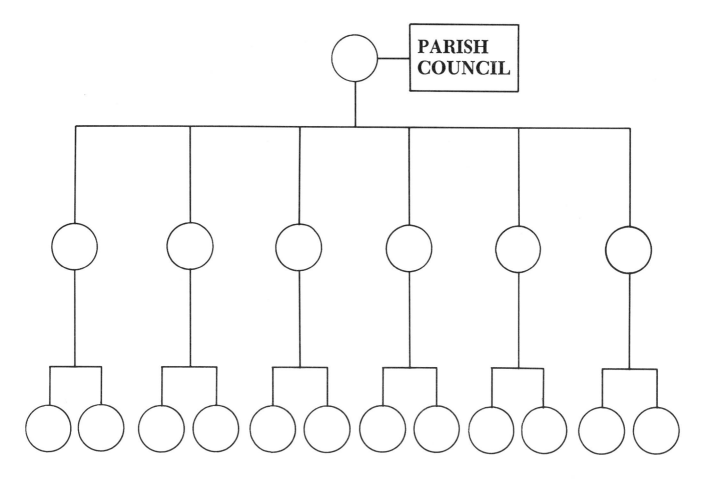

Parish Councils Were Inserted into a Hierarchic Structure

The concept of the parish council was an attempt to make way for more effective lay participation without any essential modernization, renewal or reorganization of parish structures. Simplistically conceived, the idea was to maintain the integrity of hierarchical structures while introducing a new component, the parish council, which usually would be structurally depicted as a box comprised of elected and/or selected laity with direct access to the pastor.

The Problems Which Followed

Experimentation began resulting in many struggles, hard feelings, disappointments and hardships focusing on the discovery and articulation of norms and guidelines that would define what the parish council should be and do, and how it should conduct its relationship with the pastor and parish staff, as a component of hierarchical structures. As anyone knows who worked closely with this experimentation, certain very predictable problems and tensions emerged in almost every parish council across the country, virtually without exception. The

first most predictable pitfall seemed to be the result of multiple expectations, particularly where councils and staffs began to image the role of the parish council as similar to the role of a corporate board of directors or a secular school board. Parish council members were typically invited to belong or were elected with the expectation that they were committing themselves to one meeting a month of about three hours' duration. If the pastor and the staff tried to remain faithful to their expectations of the parish council, this monthly meeting quickly multiplied into twice a month, then once a week, then twice a week, and not infrequently several times a week, until the council soon experienced burn-out, frustration, anger and exploitation, not infrequently saying, "Why do we have to do their job?" On the other hand, if the pastor and staff remained faithful to their initial request or commitment to meet once a month, the council typically accused the staff of making substantive decisions without them, "treating them like a rubber stamp," desiring their existence only as a ploy or window dressing to create the image of lay decision-making. These councils usually feel that the pastor and staff only tolerate their existence because they want them to front for unpopular decisions such as building funds, tuition increases and new buildings, etc. Either way the disillusionment and disappointment has proved more frequent than infrequent. Sometimes parish councils multiply their meetings and go through all the work of defining the problem, studying the alternatives and reaching a decision, only to find it reversed or ignored and that all their work has been in vain.

Crisis in faith and authority will occur in somewhat direct proportion to the lack of conviction that invades a people who have become incapable of doing anything of significance for themselves and others, maintaining their own sense of worth and direction by contributing to the welfare of others. However, the parish council as a vehicle for lay participation, imaged as a board of directors or secular school board, has simply failed to accomplish what it was intended to accomplish. The net result of such attempts is not a better alignment of ordained and non-ordained resources, but, rather, the very same limited and internal parochial administration experiencing non-productive tension with the parish council, and acting now more inefficiently than it did with the pastor and the staff alone.

Introducing a parish council into hierarchical structures yields a fairly predictable, informal ordering of the seven functions for which the parish council was created. Evaluation and long-range planning almost always virtually disappear. The intensive forum for complementarity between "ordained and non-ordained staff" on the one hand and the "priesthood of the laity" on the other gravitates toward latent if not blatant conflict. In what is left, there is the usual perpetual argumentation as to whether the council is policy-making or advisory and whether it should implement its own programs or aid in the delivery and implementation of other programs.

Most Success Occurred with Merged Membership

Parish councils that have worked most successfully are those that have merged the membership of staff and appointed, selected or elected laity, usually forming various committees comprised of both staff and laity to address substantial areas of the total parish life. Such councils in my experience have been as effective as they are capable of discerning a total parish vision to serve as the foundation for "common-unity" (community) and "common-union" (communion), unity of direction, purpose and action. If they do not discern and articulate an overall parish vision, then confusion will exist about the nature and purpose of the total parish, thus yielding the situation in which the respective committees

will function more effectively and with more vitality than the council as a whole. The single biggest drawback to councils, comprised of both staff and appointed, selected and elected laity, is that evaluation is usually poorly done since it is evaluation by those people reflecting on the consequences of decisions they themselves have made and actions they have taken. Also, merging staff and laity helps considerably, but it does not totally eradicate the possibility of experiencing some of the same problems and tensions of introducing a lay council into hierarchical structures.

Centrality Model Largely Fulfills Purpose of Parish Council

A centrality model and the structural reorganization that it entails accomplishes much more effectively what a parish council was intended to accomplish. It provides laity with more access to ministry and pastoral leadership. It provides on-going enrichment and support for those people assuming the responsibility for pastoral leadership in the parish, thus integrating interior and structural renewal. The centrality model provides the critically needed "middle management" while expanding the number of people involved in ministry. Many new ministry teams, responding to on-going needs, can develop and new people can be called to ministry and leadership, e.g., youth, elderly, singles, etc. Most important, however, is the fact that the centrality model appreciates the gifts of everyone, recognizing realistic limitations. It facilitates a real complementarity between "ordained and non-ordained staff" and the "priesthood of the laity," between celibate and married life styles. The centrality model completely avoids the typical checkmate structure of checks and balances established by introducing a lay council into an essentially celibate hierarchy, presuming an adversarial relationship between these two life styles and different ways of loving which is so characteristic of councils imaged as a board of directors or secular school board.

Research (Evaluation) and Development (Recommendation)
Functions within a Centrality Model

The most efficient way for integrating a parish council in a centrality model, in my opinion, is to emphasize the evaluation function, establishing the parish council as the research (evaluation) and development (recommendation) apparatus for the parish. I call this the R & D model for research and development. To activate this model, the staff, council and laity need to conceptualize and appreci-

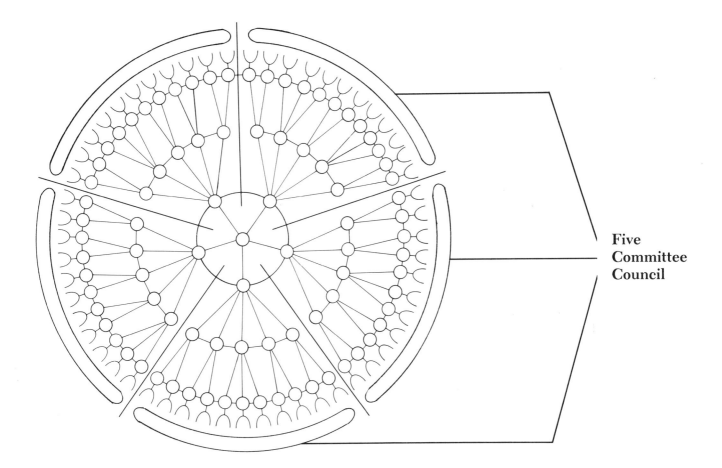

Five
Committee
Council

ate that pastoral decision-making and the implementation of these decisions is a distinctly different ministry from the ministry of evaluating and making recommendations. In this model we presume that asking the same person or persons to fulfill both functions reduces the effectiveness of each role and responsibility. Therefore, a parish should have two different groups of people.

1. Those core staff, pastoral staff, persons-in-charge, ministers, program staff and organization members who are involved in pastoral decision-making and its implementation according to their level of authority and responsibility within the centrality structure that guarantees *complementarity* among the principles of collegiality, subsidiarity, responsibility and authority, embracing laity, religious and ordained.

2. Those elected, selected and appointed persons who provide the perspective of the "person in the pew" and those with special knowledge, skills and experience—all of whom are *not* involved in pastoral decision-making and its implementation and who therefore can provide excellent, on-going, formative, objective evaluation and advisory recommendations.

Attitudinal Change Needed To Assume This Responsibility

The reorganization of the parish council to become primarily the research and development apparatus of the parish is less an issue and matter of structural transition and more a matter of attitudinal change. To accomplish this transition, the centrality model is formulated on the basis of the principles discussed previously. In short, all the primary divisions and secondary departments are formed, selecting all core staff, pastoral staff and persons-in-charge and leaving the parish council out of this reorganization. When the centrality structure is completed, the parish council is conceptualized as consisting of a number of committees, each committee having specific programs, organizations and ministry teams for which it is responsible to evaluate and make formative recommendations. The council as a whole is responsible for evaluating the total parish, vision, pastoral plan and structure annually.

The Undesirable Duality of Decision-Making Plus Evaluation and Recommendation

A more detailed explanation of the construction and operation of the R & D model will follow in the next chapter. It should be emphasized in describing the model that while the parish council and pastoral staff serve different functions, they are equally important to the overall direction of the parish. It should be said that most experienced council members, pastors and staff know in their heart-of-hearts that it is intrinsically wrong to ask the same person or persons to fulfill the two functions of decision-making and implementation on the one hand and evaluation and recommendation on the other. Not infrequently pastors, staff and council members smile, somewhat embarrassed, a kind of wry smile, in recognition that in asking people to fill both functions, you are asking them to critically challenge decisions which they themselves have made, criticize actions which they themselves have taken. Some pastors and staffs will even admit to having merged the two functions, thus inviting their would-be critics into the decision-making and implementation process, in order to defuse their criticism and formative evaluation.

Research and Development by a Council—The Sign of a Healthy Parish

In establishing the council in a research and development function, the parish obtains the benefits of an effective, independent research (evaluation) and recommendation apparatus. The parish council and its various committees are responsible for the on-going evaluation of each component of the pastoral plan and the total parish. Ultimately, the report of their findings and recommendations should be given to the pastor and core staff. These findings and recommendations can then be implemented within the appropriate component or the overall parish, at the discretion of the pastor, core staff, pastoral staff and persons-in-charge. However, the parish council as a body is not involved in the decisions to actually implement these recommendations, since their primary function is research (evaluation) and recommendation and not decision-making and pastoral implementation. Therefore, it is often the sign of a healthy parish that the pastor, core staff, pastoral staff and persons-in-charge encourage the council to utilize a public forum to report its findings and recommendations regarding the parish as a whole, or any specific organization, program or ministry team, to all parishioners through a newsletter, the bulletin, or a public meeting, or by utilizing "pulpit time," even in situations where the pastoral decision-makers and implementers will choose, for reasons which they cannot make public, not to follow the recommendations of the council.

Training for Transition

As previously mentioned, the transition from the existing roles and functions of the parish council to the research and development apparatus usually faces few structural barriers and fundamentally involves attitudinal change. This transition can best be accomplished by a well-planned developmental training effort for the benefit of the council as a whole and its various committees that focus on evaluation skills. In accomplishing the transition, existing council members should be given the opportunity to personally register their preference for functioning as a part of the decision-making and implementation apparatus of the parish or the research (evaluation) and recommendation apparatus. Thus, for example, someone may say that he or she prefers to help make the decisions and implement liturgy rather than be among those who evaluate and recommend alternative, liturgical activity. On the other hand, a person may prefer to be an evaluator and not part of the decision-making apparatus. The point is: *you can't be both!*

Assets of Reorganization for Research and Development

The assets of reorganizing the parish council to become the research and evaluation and recommending apparatus of the parish are many. The choice introduces the function of research and evaluation in the overall operation of the parish, a function that previously, for the most part, has been inoperative. The choice greatly narrows the function of the parish council, thus ensuring the likelihood that it will be productive and effective in this function. Long-range planning, implementation and decision-making are responsibilities allocated to other gifted people. The parish council and its committees become the primary source for on-going research and formative evaluation for all parish activity. Processes of decision-making and lines of accountability remain clear, separating decision-making and implementation from evaluation and recommendation. The council members, as evaluators, are not directly involved in pastoral governance and consumed with the responsibility for pastoral implementation and therefore remain in the best position to provide "objective" evaluation and recommendations.

Liabilities in Transition

Only two liabilities can be cited with regard to this transition. The first is that readjustment and retooling of the council for the evaluation role and function can produce some anxiety and tension during this period prior to training for this role. Some existing council members will, no doubt, register their preference to leave the council in order to become a core staff, pastoral staff, person-in-charge, minister or program-staff person. Secondly, elected council personnel will no longer be viewed as representing a geographical constituency in the governance of the parish. The second liability is short-lived, however, since a council person rarely, if ever, really experiences geographical constituency support. When the transition is effected, elected people will represent those interested in a particular aspect of the parish, i.e., liturgy, religious education, sacramental life and ministries of service, etc. Thus, their constituency will be based on interests and concerns rather than a geographical subdivision of the total parish boundaries.

Second Model for Integration—
Parish Council as Pastoral Staff

A second model for integrating an existing council with a centrality structure is to construct the centrality structure in a way that makes the pastoral staff and the parish council the same body.

Each member of the parish council in this format is responsible for setting policy and making decisions appropriate to the "department" he or she is responsible for coordinating. The emphasis in this restructuring is primarily on decision-making, and secondarily on implementation. Although it is conceivable to hope that the council will retain the functions of long-range planning and/or evaluation in this restructuring, in fact experience proves that these two functions will greatly diminish for lack of adequate time.

Reorganization for Second Model

In a reorganization that follows this choice, the council comprises the entire pastoral staff and usually the committees of the council consisting of approximately five pastoral staff per division (a committee for each division) or a committee comprised of all the persons-in-charge constituting a particular department. This P.I.C. variation makes the council committees primarily responsible for decision-making and implementation of the various programs, ministry teams and organizations and the total council responsible for the overall pastoral plan of the parish.

Structural Shifts—For the Second Model

The transition to this model usually requires considerable structural and organizational shifting. Council personnel who are not already functioning as pastoral staff and/or persons-in-charge must be selected, authorized and formed to fulfill these responsibilities and functions. The council and its various committees would necessarily need to be intimately involved in (or apprised of) the process of discerning, articulating and proclaiming the parish vision as well as the development of the parish's pastoral plan.

Immediate and Long-Term Gains and Losses of This Model

The only asset of this kind of restructuring is the immediate gain obtained by limiting the functions of the parish council, actively emphasizing their involvement in decision-making according to the level of responsibility and their high involvement in actual pastoral implementation. The long-term losses and liabilities of this kind of reorganization far outnumber its initial attributes and gains. Evaluation of existing activities virtually disappears, and in those rare instances where it is done, it is done poorly because it is done by the same people actually making the decisions and implementing the activity being evaluated. Since almost all council members are elected and presumed to represent geographical constituencies, factionalism and bias are likely to become factors in allocating resources and implementing programs. If council members continue to be elected there would arise a dysfunctional tension between the pastor and the pastoral authority of the core staff and the pastoral staff and persons-in-charge, since it is grossly unfair to presume that an elective process could or would guarantee a good working relationship between "middle management" and the pastor and core staff. As a result, either the elective process will be abandoned or "middle management" will be ineffectual. The number of components (ministry teams, programs and organizations) will be limited by the number of people willing to run for the parish council, and an immense dysfunctional conflict and tension will arise between the pastor and core staff on the one hand, and the "middle management" pastoral staff and persons-in-charge on the other as to who works for whom. This tension will be particularly pronounced and experienced in parishes where the persons-in-charge previously imaged themselves as a board of directors or something analogous to a secular school board.

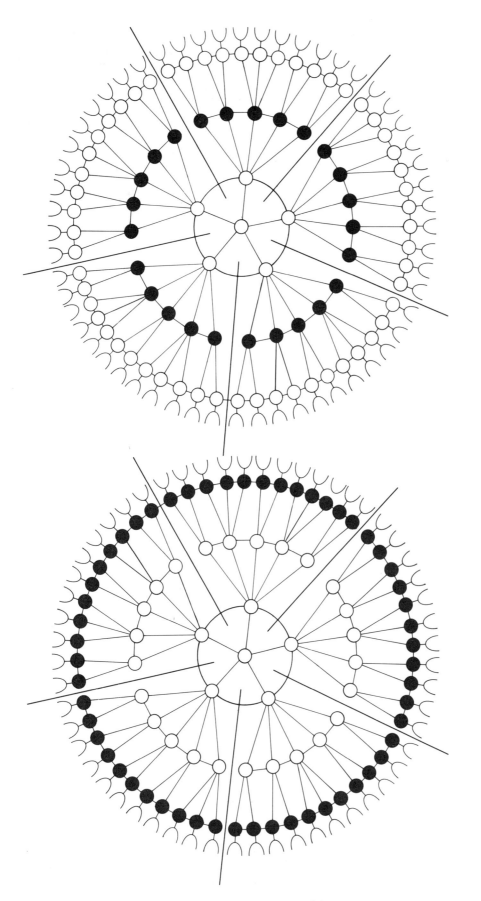

**Parish Council
as
Pastoral Staff**

**Parish Council
as
Persons-In-Charge**

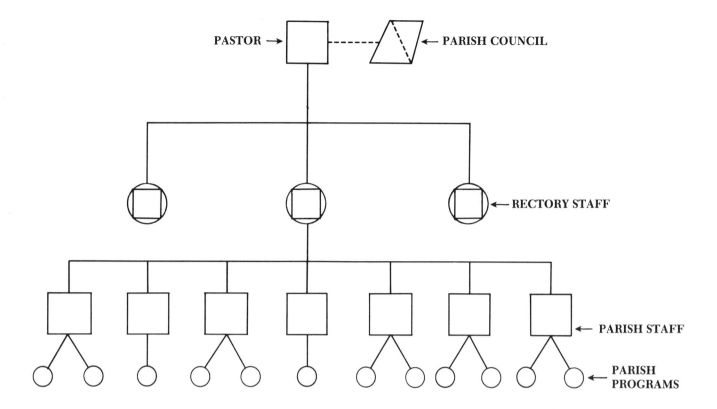

PASTOR → □ -------- ◹ ← PARISH COUNCIL

← RECTORY STAFF

← PARISH STAFF

← PARISH PROGRAMS

The "Two-Hats" Model of Integrating a Parish Council with a Centrality Model

Numerous structural reorganizations have been attempted combining the role and functions of the parish council with regard to decision-making, implementation and evaluation. All of these experiments subsequently and repeatedly proved the necessity of integrating decision-making and implementation. Simply stated, people shouldn't participate in decision-making unless they will be participating in some degree in implementing the consequences of those decisions. The best level for making a decision is that level within the structure that most adequately involves those persons who will be responsible for implementing the decision. This same experimentation repeatedly proves the incapability and undesirability of expecting the same people to wear the *two hats* of decision maker-implementer and evaluator-recommender. No matter how a parish structures and deploys its resources, if it expects some people to wear both of these hats, invariably and inevitably they will wear one extremely poorly. The one usually tossed aside and discarded first is evaluation. Even structural reorganization, which emphasizes training in research and evaluation skills and knowledge, proves futile when people are expected to wear both hats. Even though the argument can be presented that those

making the decisions and implementing the decisions are closest to the problems at hand and therefore should be the best evaluators, the theory proves groundless when it is structurally effected. People who make decisions and implement activities based on these decisions cannot avoid becoming emotionally invested in their efforts. This investment makes them incapable of dispassionate, effective, formative evaluation.

The Worst But Most Popular Model— Parish Council as Board of Directors

The worst, most dysfunctional model for structuring a parish council is to image it as analogous to a board of directors or a secular school board within a hierarchical structure.

Although it is the worst of all possible alternatives, it should be commented upon simply because it is the most popularly selected alternative in spite of its consistent and overwhelming failure in virtually every parish in almost all dioceses throughout the world. It continues to be tried and it continues to fail because parishes don't know how to reorganize on the basis of centrality structure. It is odd and amazing to realize how consistently and inevitably this model fails only to be tried again somewhere else. The reason for this dilemma is simple: every time it fails, its failure is attributed to the personality (or lack of personality) of the pastor or the personalities of the council rather than appreciating the structural reasons that doom this alternative to failure even before it begins. The hierarchical model almost always begins with the expectation that the council will serve as an advisory board, think-tank and brain-trust, offering recommendations and advice to the pastor. In time the pastor usually withdraws and abdicates his prerogatives, charging the council with primary pastoral responsibility. Some dioceses have guidelines which actually provide for this transition. However, in most dioceses the transition occurs in parishes contrary to specific guidelines limiting parish councils to the advisory and recommending function.

Why the Worst of All Models Persists!

Probably most councils, constituted and organized into a hierarchical structure, began to image themselves as a board of directors or secular school board simply because they didn't have any other image or model to turn to as long as parish structures continued to be viewed hierarchically. Councils felt the need to make decisions which they believed the pastor and staff were incapable of making due to a lack of knowledge and skills or attitudinal bias that did not really appreciate the real problems of marriage and family life. Eventually they came to behave as a board of directors even though they weren't stockholders, or as a secular school board in spite of the fact that they did not have the authority to levy taxes invested in secular school boards.

In this option, the entire staff is viewed as hierarchically structured from the pastor (at the top) down to the heads of the various programs, organizations and ministry teams. The council views itself as a lateral appendage to the pastor—in effect, as a "board of directors" and as such empowered to evaluate, set policy, make decisions and set priorities that effect the implementation of efforts in which they are usually not involved. Their primary role is that of decision-maker, policy-maker and priority-setter.

The only asset attributed to this model is that it does provide a limited forum for the participation of a few laity in parish governance to the extent that the pastor shares or abdicates his prerogatives. The liabilities are many. First of all, it causes inevitable latent or blatant, unproductive conflict and tension between the elected council and "ordained and non-ordained" staff. It usually presumes an unnecessarily adversarial and uncomplementary relationship between married and celibate life styles that requires checkmating and balance. It yields a de-

feated, often passive staff or frustrated council experiencing that they are either overworked or being utilized as a rubber stamp for window dressing. Often the staff perceives the council as adding more red tape and confusion to an already overwhelming workload. This leads to a more limited and internal parochial administration that operates with more inefficiency than did the pastor and staff when they worked alone, unhampered by the parish council. It creates a false image of lay participation and constituency representation; in fact, most parish councils would readily admit that they lack a constituency and feel very much out of touch with the rest of the parishioners. It confuses the functions of recommendation, decision-making, implementation and evaluation in an indistinct, wholistic aspiration to execute all functions, condemning the council to failure in most, if not all, of what it hopes to accomplish. If the council and its committees become heavily involved in implementing specific components of the pastoral plan, each committee inevitably narrows its concern and the council as a whole loses its ability to view and benefit the parish as a whole. Evaluation and long-range planning, in particular, quickly emerge as luxuries among the multiple burdensome functions and are done very poorly, if indeed they are done at all.

Summary and Concluding Remarks

In summary and in conclusion, I have presented the essential alternatives for the functioning of the parish council. Three of these alternatives involve integrating the parish council with a centrality model. Of these three I have recommended most the R & D model, presenting also the assets, liabilities and transitional difficulties of the other two methods for integrating a parish council with a centrality structure. I have also cited at length the assets and liabilities of viewing the parish council as something analogous to a board of directors or secular school board in hierarchically structured parishes.

This does not mean that these are the only specific alternatives which are variations of the primary options I have presented. The first three models are compatible with the centering model of parish governance. The fourth model, even though it is most typical in many parishes, does not allow the full potential of a parish council to be realized nor does it provide a springboard for significant structural reorganization that enables the complementarity between the principles of collegiality, authority and subsidiarity. In fact, the fourth model, viewing the parish council as something analogous to a board of directors or secular school board, can actually provide a barrier to structural reorganization that centers authority, makes accountability mutual and provides access to pastoral leadership and ministry for most parishioners. Yet some councils and staffs may choose to retain and maintain the fourth model, with all its limitations, thus perpetuating the very same isolation from pastoral leadership and ministry experienced by most laity that occasioned Vatican II in the first place. Sometimes the decision to delay structural reorganization on the basis of the centrality model is the right one as long as those making the decisions know and appreciate the alternatives open to them and the purpose for their delay.

Chapter Ten
The Functioning of a Parish Council in a Research and Development Role

Recommendation and evaluation comprise the two primary functions and form the basic purpose of a parish council whose fundamental interest is on-going research and development. It is only through effective evaluation of the global parish efforts and the respective activities of various organizations, ministry teams and programs that a parish can gain insight into what to correct and how to correct it in order to achieve its goals. It is truly unfortunate that the role of evaluation and the benefits of evaluation somehow are the first to be pushed on the "back burner" by parishioners attempting to fulfill multiple functions.

Reason for Poor Organizational Operation

Many parishes, of course, don't undertake on-going evaluation because they really don't know what they are trying to be and do. Such parishes can't or won't invest in discerning, articulating and planning what it is they are about, operating on the unspoken principle: "If you don't know where you are going, you can't possibly get lost." However, even becoming clear about the direction the parish aspires to move in cannot by itself guarantee that it will successfully arrive at and accomplish what it hopes to accomplish. One of the basic reasons for poor organizational operation and constant emphasis on dealing with crisis after crisis is the feeling that we are standing still, spinning our wheels and getting nowhere. This is simply because the values of on-going research (evaluation) and development (recommendations) have not been appreciated and

internalized by the Catholic parish. No other collective endeavor, no other human enterprise of comparable magnitude, involving so many people and the expenditure of so much money, would dare to persist without the benefits of on-going research (evaluation) and development (recommendations). Furthermore, any follow-up planning or problem-solving is virtually blind and arbitrary without the benefits of at least minimal research (evaluation) and formative recommendations from a source not initially or primarily responsible for the activities being evaluated.

The Parish Council Is Best Suited for the Ministry of Formative Evaluation and Recommendations

Good evaluation is effective evaluation, evaluation that makes a difference! Effective evaluation takes time and effort and is true to the proverb, "You only get out of it what you put into it." While good evaluation procedures and proper reporting of recommendations do require time, care and effort, they do not have to be terribly complex processes. Evaluation procedures should certainly not become bogged down in statistical comparisons and trend analysis which become meaningless or so far removed from practical application that the results tend to get shelved or just plain disregarded.

As a parish engages in renewal, discerning, articulating and proclaiming a unifying vision, it improves its pastoral plan and develops new organizational structures. As such a parish expands pastoral leadership, the number of people in pastoral ministry, and improves communication, accountability and the delegation of responsibility, formalized apparatus for evaluation and recommendation becomes even more critical. In most parishes, the parish council is most suited to carry out these research (evaluation) and development (recommendation) functions for the benefit of the parish.

In the generation since Vatican II the call for the involvement of laity in sharing responsibility for the growth and development of the local church has certainly increased. Responding to this challenge by making a commitment to critically needed, on-going, formative evaluation and recommendation is certainly just as much a ministry as commitment to participate in the pastoral leadership of a new or existing organization, program or ministry team.

Prerequisites If the Council Is To Embrace This Ministry

In order that a parish council assume the responsibility for being the research and development apparatus of a parish, we must presume that the parish, first of all, has accomplished sufficient renewal to yield a discerned, articulated, proclaimed and affirmed parish vision. Second, we presume that this parish has effectively evaluated its pastoral plan in light of that vision and changed how the staff spend their time individually and collectively as a result of this process. Third, we presume that the parish has successfully reorganized its structures for communication, accountability and collegiality. This presupposes that the exercise of pastoral authority and the delegation of responsibility have successfully attained an operative structure of core staff, pastoral staff and persons-in-charge. This presumes also that divisional and departmental integrity have been achieved so that the structure operates with a healthy regular rhythm of meetings for individual support and supervision as well as collective meetings which guarantee the collegiality necessary to support, empower, and therefore undergird the exercise of authority.

Complementary but Different Ministries

With the preceding prerequisites accomplished, the responsibility for decision-making, direction-setting, priority-setting and the exercise of pastoral authority remains the prerogative of the pastor, core staff, pastoral staff and persons-in-charge and the various ministers, staff and membership comprising the various components of the overall pastoral plan, i.e., programs, organizations, ministry teams, etc.

For the parish council most effectively to fulfill its function as researcher (evaluator) and developer (recommender), thereby installing it as the R & D (Research and Development) apparatus for the parish, it is *absolutely imperative* to remember that while the parish council (evaluators and recommenders) and the parish staff (decision-makers and pastoral implementers) serve different functions, they are equally important to the overall direction and development of the parish. The parish council is responsible for researching (evaluating) and development (making recommendations) bearing on each and every program, organization and ministry team within the parish and provides the same function with regard to the parish as a whole.

The parish council must therefore reorganize itself into divisions, committees or units in order to render itself capable of covering all of the various components of the pastoral plan in addition to providing divisional and departmental evaluations and recommendations where desirable. For example, the council could establish one committee for evaluating all organizations, programs and ministry teams affecting liturgical vitality and worship and that whole division if it happens to be a division within the centrality structure. Another committee may be charged with evaluating all those components relating to religious education or religious and academic education, etc.

Recommendations That May or May Not Be Implemented

Whereas the responsibility of the pastor, core staff, pastoral staff, persons-in-charge, the ministers of ministry teams, membership of organizations and program staff is decision-making that leads ultimately to implementation, the responsibility of the parish council is to evaluate and make decisions pertaining to recommendations that may or may not ultimately be implemented. They are not responsible for implementation and therefore should not expect that their recommendations will inevitably be implemented. The parish council providing research and development for a parish ultimately reports its findings and recommendations to the pastor, core staff, pastoral staff, persons-in-charge, ministers, program-staff and all members to whom their findings and recommendations pertain. They may even have a public forum for registering their evaluative comments and recommendations to the parish as a whole, but at no time should they expect that the decision-makers and implementers of the parish are compelled to act on their recommendations.

Problematic of Meshing Management and Evaluation

In any comparable corporate or collective enterprise of the equivalent size of most Catholic parishes, it is taken for granted that "management" is not bound to accept the evaluation of the research and development resources at face value, nor is it bound to implement the recommendations totally or even partially. Management is, of course, bound to consider the evaluation and recommendations sincerely, seriously and with the utmost respect. This normative separation between the ultimate role of responsibility and function of decision-makers and implementers versus evaluators and recommenders is maintained to ensure the integrity and maximum effectiveness of both groups respectively. If management were bound to take all the evaluative comments at face value and implement all the recommendations accordingly, the function of those providing research and development would be management and not research and development. If this unhealthy and unwise meshing of roles, responsibilities and functions is allowed to occur, then future evaluation and recommendations diminish in value and become ineffectual because their subsequent efforts will be researching and evaluating the consequences of decisions they themselves have made.

Essential Separation of Functions

At the risk of being redundant, since it is so important, it must be remembered that the function of pastoral decision-makers and implementers is the ministry of management and the proper implementation of ministerial resources. The ministry of the council fulfilling the function of research and development is to offer quality evaluations and recommendations to be embraced and implemented at the discretion of the pastor, core staff, pastoral staff, persons-in-charge, the ministers, staff and membership comprising the various ministry teams, programs and various organizations. The council *is not* involved in pastoral decision-making except for that decision-making which shapes its evaluation and recommendations.

The council is the single locus for coordinating research and development to embrace all levels of parish reality—single ministry teams, programs, organizations, departments, divisions and the parish as a whole. This separation of functions guarantees that the evaluation and recommendations forthcoming will be as "objective" as possible. Actually, such evaluation can never be utterly "objective." By "objective" one can only guarantee as much as possible

that "subjective" judgment is the ministry of those having no vested interest which would lead them to be overly critical or overly tolerant of how human and financial resources are being utilized.

Parish Council's Direct Accountability to the Pastor

For the council as a whole and its various committees, divisions or departments to maintain objectivity in evaluation and recommendations, the council must be viewed and organized as *highly autonomous*. Following the model of most organizations of comparable size, a council fulfilling the R & D function will probably be autonomous of all pastoral authority except for accountability through its own head directly to the pastor. Of course, the various committees and departments comprising the council as a whole will have to seek information and work collaboratively with core staff, pastoral staff, persons-in-charge and the various ministry teams, programs and organizations in order to carry out their roles and functions most effectively.

Reverent, Not Adversative Relationship Between Management and Evaluators

What has been said up to this point about the independent functions of "management" versus evaluators and recommenders and the need to reverence their respective integrity and mutual autonomy (in spite of the fact that each group depends upon the other to do its own ministry most effectively) should not be construed to presume that it is necessary, wise or desirable to promote a hostile relationship between these two essential ministries. Those involved in evaluation and making recommendations are not the adversaries or the enemies of those charged with the responsibility of effective pastoral decision-making and implementation. Similarly, those involved in pastoral decision-making and its implementation should not view the ministry of research and development with enmity. On the contrary, a conciliatory attitude and mutual cooperation will help both to better fulfill their own ministry. If management helps those involved in research and development to perform their ministry conscientiously and effectively, the result will be more effective, wiser pastoral decisions and better implementation. The more help those providing the ministry of research and development can give to management, the easier and more effective will be their own ministry of providing fruitful research, effective evaluation and insightful recommendations. If one group tries to thwart the effective ministry of the other or if they mutually assume an antagonistic relationship, each group will find their ministry much more difficult, much less effective and both will lose as a result. Perhaps even more important, the parish will lose.

Precise Definitions of Evaluation

Having used the terms "research" and "evaluation" repeatedly to explain the research-development model, it seems appropriate to define precisely what "evaluation" means.

1. *Purpose Evaluation—Why?* Briefly stated, this means that activity undertaken to ascertain the value of purpose and aspirations. It is concerned with closing the gap between where the parish *is* and where it *is called* to be.

2. *Outcome Evaluation—What?* Briefly stated, this means that activity undertaken to compare existing declared objectives and anticipated outcomes with actual, tangible outcomes and results. These may be compared with alternative objectives for attaining the same or other outcomes.

3. *Process Evaluation—How?* Briefly stated, this means that activity which compares and contrasts the effectiveness and efficiency of alternative means for attaining a desired objective, outcome and result.

The Four Target Areas To Be Evaluated

Using this definition, the parish council and its committees, seeking to provide the research and development function for a parish, will need to turn their *purpose, outcome* and *process* evaluation efforts toward four major areas in the parish.

1. The parish as a whole, including its vision, overall pastoral plan and structure for effective communication, accountability, pastoral leadership, collegiality and delegation of responsibility. In evaluating the overall structure it would, of course, evaluate the effectiveness of various management levels including different divisions and departments.

2. Each parish organization which is part of the pastoral plan and tied into the parish through the structure for communication and delegated responsibility, i.e., St. Vincent de Paul Society, Men's Club, Altar and Rosary Society, Festival Committee, etc.

3. Each program which is a part of the parish's pastoral plan, for example, parish school, Genesis II, Marriage Preparation Program, C.C.D., T.E.C., Christ Renews His Parish, Renew, etc.

4. Each ministry team which is part of the pastoral plan and tied into the parish structure of accountability and communication, i.e., different ministries of care, Hospital Visitation Team, Welcoming Ministry Team, Liturgy Team, Marriage Enrichment Team, etc.

Expanding the Description of the Three Levels of Evaluation

Keeping these four different areas in mind, it is possible to expand the description of the three primary levels of evaluation (and ensuing recommendations) to be touched on in the evaluation of the parish as a whole (including the various departments and divisions): the various organizations, the various programs and the various ministry teams. The three primary levels of evaluation correspond to three simple questions: "Why?" "What?" "How?"

First Level: The Issue of Purpose—The Question of "Why?"

The first level of evaluation embraces the issue of purpose, vision and aspirations, whether evaluating the parish as a whole, a department, a division or organization, a program or a ministry team. It remains of continuing importance to recurringly ask, "Why does this exist? Why does this parish as a whole need to exist now? Has anything changed substantially in the composition of the community or with regard to neighboring parishes which changes or alters the purpose for which this parish exists? At this point in time, why does this parish need a particular division or department? Has anything changed to alter substantially the need or purpose of any existing organization? Is an existing program needed less, as much or more than it was previously? Has any particular ministry team outlived its need or has anything changed presenting a good argument that it expand or narrow its purpose?"

Parishes exist in neighborhoods and in social communities experiencing rapidly changing sociological characteristics and needs. Therefore, it is a tremendous mistake to presume that simply because something was needed once or created to meet a specific purpose, nothing will change affecting that need and altering that purpose. Researching and evaluating why a parish exists or why any component of the total parish exists is by no means a futile waste of time. It is, on the contrary, organizationally and pastorally irresponsible not to address this first level of evaluation recurringly.

Second Level: The Issues of Objectives and Outcomes—The Question of "What?"

The second level of evaluation addresses the question "What?" Apart and aside from the purpose and aspirations which define the reason for being of the parish as a whole—its various divisions and departments and its various organizations, programs and ministry teams—what are the desired outcomes, goals or objectives, the actual results and the real tangible outcomes of these endeavors? Is an organization, program, ministry team, department or division providing what it is supposed to provide or is there substantial discrepancy between what it is actually producing in comparison with what it espouses to provide? Are the real outcomes in fact more beneficial than the espoused objectives or do the espoused objectives simply mask and hide substantial poverty in the real outcomes as these relate to the espoused objectives? In addressing this level, evaluators are seeking to find out what the parish as a whole or any of its parts is doing and what are the results of this effort.

Third Level: The Issue of Process—The Question of "How?"

The third level of evaluation is concerned with the activity, structural barriers and processes that are part of a parish's daily and weekly rhythm. This level of evaluation asks the question "How?" Whereas the first two levels addressing "Why?" and "What?" deal with espoused purpose, desired outcome and actual results, the third level covers all activity that professional evaluators call "process evaluation." It concerns itself with the emotional climate of the parish as a whole, various divisions, departments, organizations, programs and ministry teams. In doing process evaluation, researchers are concerned with how effectively and efficiently problems get identified, alternatives are generated, and decisions are made and implemented. In summary, it partly involves an evaluation of the problem-solving process and the quality of the conduct by which an organization, ministry team, program, department, division or the parish as a whole continuously clarifies its direction.

Process evaluation is concerned with the quality of interaction between and among members, staff and ministers of various organizations, programs, and ministry teams, as well as with the quality of relationship and collaboration between and among organizations, programs, ministry teams, departments and divisions comprising the total parish. In researching and evaluating the quality of relationships, researchers concern themselves with how well differences, conflicts and tensions are utilized and how the climate affects the productive expression of new ideas, feelings and values. The development of commitment and the quality of resources for developing the knowledge, skills and attitudes of pastoral leaders, ministers, staff and the membership of various committees and organizations also comes within their scope. Process evaluation, in summary, concerns itself with how a particular group or the parish as a whole goes about being and doing that which it is being and doing in order to produce definite results in pursuit of its espoused objectives and aspirations—the very purpose for which it exists.

Parishes Are Pregnant with Discrepancies Between Purpose, Objectives and Outcome

The first two levels of evaluation addressing the questions "Why?" and "What?" deal primarily with the value and comparative value of *espoused purpose* and *desired versus real outcomes*. Since both questions are asked, this form of evaluation provides the instrument for evaluating any discrepancies among espoused purpose, desired outcome and what, in fact, is being delivered. Many Catholic parishes are pregnant with existing organizations, programs and ministry teams that continue to conduct their activity long after the need and purpose which legitimized their existence has disappeared. Catholic parishes are even more plagued with a multitude of organizations, programs and ministry teams requiring considerable human and financial resources. Year after year they go through considerable motions making it obvious to everyone that there is almost no existing relationship between their espoused purpose and reason for being, their declared objectives and the tangible results of their efforts. It is virtually irresponsible to permit such tremendous waste on the basis of the often articulated excuse that parishes, with their divisions, departments, organizations, programs and ministry teams, are doing something that "cannot be measured." While it is true that effects can't always be weighed in ounces or grams or measured in inches and feet, the effects of any human endeavor can be ascertained in some measure, often making glaringly obvious any discrepancy between purpose and declared objective—and the tangible outcome!

Distinction Between Process and Outcome Evaluation

Purpose and outcome evaluation addressing the questions "Why?" and "What?" help to develop judgments and decisions about the comparative worth of efforts and how well aligned are espoused purpose, declared objectives and actual results. "Process evaluation" sharpens the judgments and decisions needed to improve the quality of directedness and the quality of relationships affecting outcome. Process evaluation embraces the issues of efficiency and the effectiveness of means. Outcome evaluation addresses the effectiveness and productivity of results occurring as a result of those activities.

Process Evaluation and Means—End—Continuity

Many parishes recognize the on-going need for process evaluation as well as purpose evaluation and outcome evaluation for addressing the question "How?" as well as the questions "Why?" and "What?" for two obvious reasons. The first is that many organizations, ministry teams and programs need support from an on-going evaluation of how they go about achieving their results. Second, and perhaps more important, *process evaluation, purpose evaluation* and *outcome evaluation* are needed to research and evaluate *Means—End—Continuity.* In short, are the means consistent with the results to be obtained? Pastors and parish staffs observe a multitude of instances in which organizations, ministry teams and programs deploy means and engage in activity that is totally contrary to the results they say they are trying to obtain. In these instances it is not at all uncommon to understand and explain why the actual consequences and results of an endeavor are contrary to its declared objectives. Often, what is actually being achieved clearly reflects the means and activities employed with total disregard of the espoused purpose and declared objectives.

Summary of Evaluation Matrix

The following evaluation matrix summarizes the three levels of evaluation addressing the three questions "Why?" "What?" and "How?" and the four different areas toward which research and development (evaluation and recommendations) are directed. It is worth repeating that ministry teams, programs and the parish as a whole need and deserve the support of a group of people whose ministry it is to help them (continuously) address these questions. Having a group of people who minister by providing on-going research and development (evaluation and recommendations) does not mean the installation of a hostile group. On the contrary, such a group will quickly befriend pastoral leaders, ministers, staff and organizational membership utilizing their skills and their "objective indifference"

to further author, empower and guarantee effective leadership and ministry.

These preceding comments have laid the foundation, theory, rationale, purpose and value for having a group of people in a parish whose ministry is to provide the function of on-going research (evaluation) and development (recommendations). In the preceding comments it was specifically recommended that the parish council is the ideal group to assume this responsibility. Before stipulating step-by-step how the parish council could go about assuming the responsibility of providing this role, a few additional comments should be made about the composition of the parish council and its various committees as it prepares to embrace this responsibility.

A Transition Time—Ministry Options

When the transition to research and development is undertaken, existing members of the parish council should be permitted to register a preference as to whether they prefer to minister through pastoral decision-making and implementation or pastoral research and development. If they prefer the function of the former ministry, they should be encouraged to withdraw from the parish council and, where possible, to assume responsibility as a core staff, pastoral staff, person-in-charge, etc.

Election to Parish Council with R & D Emphasis

Election to the parish council is an ideal procedure for building a membership of those who will provide the research and development function, but it should not become the only avenue providing access to this ministry. In fact, election of members of the parish council whose primary function is research and development makes a great deal more sense than an election procedure for a council emphasizing any other function. Parishioners are delighted by the opportunity to elect people providing the perspective of the "person-in-the-pew" for the on-going research (evaluation) and development (recommendations) of the parish as a whole and its respective programs, organizations and ministry teams. As parishioners become more aware of the new function and responsibility of the parish council, the more concerned they will be to elect people on the basis of their general and specific evaluative skills. Parishioners will then, of course, be less concerned with the neighborhood or area of the parish in which these elected people reside. They will certainly not want people with any "bone to pick" who may hinder the council from providing anything but

EVALUATION MATRIX

THREE LEVELS OF EVALUATION		AREAS TO EVALUATE			
		Parish as a whole Intra & Inter Divisional & Departmental	Organizations	Programs	Teams Ministry
First	Why—asks and answers the question(s) of purpose, need and aspirations	Purpose Evaluation			
Second	What—asks and answers the question(s) of declared objectives, outcome, results and effects	Objective and Outcome Evaluation			
Third	How—asks and answers the question(s) of process, activity, means and climate	Process Evaluation			

the most objective and "wholly indifferent" evaluation and recommendations.

Invitation of Experts to Parish Council

In addition to elected people, it would be a mistake to refrain from the opportunity to invite "experts," i.e., people with special knowledge and skills who could team up with elected membership to guarantee not only the perspective of the "person-in-the-pew" but the "professional" perspective as well. For example, in evaluating the school, why not invite professional educators and administrators to aid the effort of the elected members of the council? In evaluating liturgy and worship, why not invite professional musicians, artists, etc.? If a committee of the council is evaluating a ministry team charged with the responsibility of long-range planning, why not invite parishioners to help elected council members evaluate the effectiveness and efficiency of the planning? Some parishioners have invaluable knowledge about the community and the sociological trends affecting the secular community in which the parish is embedded.

Consultative Resources—Wise Investment

Frequently it is wise, yet inexpensive, to invest a nominal amount of money to obtain consultative resources to help the parish council (both elected and selected membership) develop skills in providing effective research (evaluation) and development (recommendations). Usually these consultative resources will be experts in program or systems evaluation or may be people charged with the responsibility of providing on-going research and development for secular organizations of comparable size. The steps in organizing, preparing and implementing a parish council to provide this research and development function are as follows:

Step I: Organizing the Parish Council To Provide the Research and Development Function by Doing Evaluation and Making Recommendations

1. *Obtaining Parish's Corporate Challenge, Pastoral Plan and Centrality Structure*—The Council must begin by requesting and obtaining the parish's articulated vision (corporate challenge). The council needs the parish's pastoral plan which should include the information pertaining to how many staff and how much staff time has been allocated to various programs, ministry teams, organizations, committees, etc. Finally, the council will need a complete visual presentation of the parish centrality structure including divisional and departmental

boundaries and the names of people already appointed to core staff, pastoral staff and persons-in-charge positions. Also, the council will need the names of the staff, ministers and membership who comprise the various programs, ministry teams and parish organizations. All of this information will provide the council with the basic information concerning the purpose of the parish, the pastoral plan through which the parish fulfills that purpose, and a description of the structure for communication, accountability, collegiality and pastoral leadership—the broadest, basic information and the "Why?" "What?" and "How?" of the parish.

2. Assess Priorities of Roles and Functions—In order to be true to itself, the parish council must first assess its present priorities of roles and functions, divesting itself of conflicting activities and/or other activities that will overburden the council and prevent it from effectively assuming this role of research and development. Thus the council should divest itself of policy-making and pastoral decision-making, from the implementation of programs, and from long-range planning.

3. Review of Present Committee and Parish Structures—The council should review its present committee structure, adding elected and/or non-elected resources to ensure that its own structure sufficiently overlaps, encompasses and embraces the parish structure for communication, leadership, collegiality, accountability and implementation. This should then provide research (evaluation) and development (recommendations) addressing the total parish, its respective divisions and departments and the various programs, ministry teams and organizations. This will require a review of the parish structure and a familiarity with decisions regarding the high priority components, i.e., components of strategy in implementation and not just planning stages.

4. Evaluation and Projection of Time Lines—The council and its respective committees will need to evaluate the time available to fulfill their functions, projecting time lines that set aside an adequate amount of time in the course of a year for beginning, working up and ending its evaluation and determining, articulating and communicating its recommendations.

5. Assigning Committee Heads and Establishing a Meetings Calendar—The parish council should designate an individual to be responsible for each of the various committees, and, of course, someone

must be appointed, designated, chosen or selected to lead the entire parish council. The heads of the various committees should establish a calendar in advance for meeting together with the leader of the council who, incidentally, should not be burdened with the dual responsibility of also being a committee head. A regular rhythm should be established in advance for individual committee meetings, for meetings of the council as a whole and for regular meetings between the pastor and the head of the parish council. It should not be necessary, nor is it advisable, to establish a regular rhythm of meetings of the council as a whole or of all committee heads where the pastor is expected to be present, except at special meetings for the purpose of reporting recommendations.

6. Council's Maintenance of Its Integrity—The council as a whole should not lose sight of its responsibility to maintain its own overall integrity. Even though it will probably be a committee of the council evaluating and preparing the recommendations for a division or a department and specific organizations, programs and ministry teams, the evaluation and recommendations should come from the council as a whole. In short, the entire council is responsible for *all* evaluations and recommendations. The responsibility for ensuring a good working relationship between the council and those responsible for pastoral decision-making and implementation rests ultimately with two people—the pastor and the person-in-charge of the council. Just as the pastor receives information from core staff in relationship to pastoral staff who are in relationship with persons-in-charge and so on, so should the head of the council develop an interdependent relationship with committee heads and sub-committee heads, etc., ensuring the organizational integrity, lines of communication, accountability, collegiality and authority for research and development.

Step II: Preparing for Evaluation
1. *Resolution to Evaluate the Parish in Whole and Then in Part*—Generally speaking, the best overall procedure for evaluating purpose, outcome and process is to begin with the resolution to evaluate the whole, and then its parts in light of the whole, and then the parts of parts, and so on. Therefore, a council should begin with a determination to evaluate and make recommendations regarding the "Why?" "What?" and "How?" focusing on the whole parish, then utilizing its committee structure to narrow the focus to address various divisions, departments and finally all specific organizations, pro-

grams and ministry teams. Having done this at least once, a second cycle can proceed in the opposite direction, i.e., from parts to the whole. However, a procedure that focuses on the whole and concerns itself with the constituent parts should be repeated at least every two years, eighteen months or annually, even if the reverse procedure is to be undertaken in between this cycle.

2. *Evaluate: Why?" Then "What?" Then "How?" Personalities: Never!*—The council as a whole and its various committees should reverence the intrinsic value of focusing its evaluation and reporting its recommendations, beginning with the question "Why?" then advancing to the question "What?" and finally addressing the questions, concerns and issues related to "How?" It is a virtual waste of time to reverse the order of addressing these questions and their related concerns and issues. It is futile to undertake a "process evaluation" before completing an adequate "outcome evaluation" or to undertake the latter before completing an evaluation of "purpose."

It is never appropriate for research and development resources to evaluate and make recommendations regarding specific personalities of the personnel responsible for pastoral decision-making and its implementation. Personnel evaluations are the responsibility of pastoral implementers to whom they are accountable. Of course, good research and development will aid pastoral leaders to fulfill this responsibility which is theirs, but it should never become the formal or informal responsibility of those whose ministry is research and development.

As a matter of fact, Catholic parishes are plagued universally by repetitiously erring on this account. I have witnessed more frequently than infrequently parish councils trying to do evaluation together with decision-making, implementing and long-range planning, making a conscious choice to evaluate personnel, e.g., principal, director of religious education, youth minister, associate, pastor, etc. Such evaluation is not only ineffective; it is terribly unjust and unkind to presume the authority and responsibility to evaluate personnel, unaware of purpose, desired outcomes and results, or process, and without their having contributed any evaluation or recommendations regarding purpose, objectives, consequences or process. At the same time, this error totally destroys the integrity of pastoral leadership by immensely confusing accountability, prerogatives for hiring, firing and leadership.

3. *Developing an Evaluation Schedule*—The council as a whole should develop an evaluation and recommendation schedule preliminarily specifying for each level of evaluation "Why?" "What?" and "How?" and the focus of evaluation (whole parish, divisions, departments, organizations, programs and ministry teams), the dates and time-lines for beginning, conducting and completing the evaluative and recommendation activities. This schedule should specify adequate time for interviewing, collection and collating pertinent information, discussing data, articulating conclusions, discussing alternative recommendations and writing a report of evaluation and recommendation. The schedule must allow adequate time for processing committee and sub-committee reports through the whole council. Time must be allocated for preparing written and verbal reports for the pastoral leadership and, sometimes, the parish as a whole.

4. *Initial Limitation of Focus and Levels*—Frequently the council will not be adequately staffed or prepared to cover every focus and every level in the first year. Decisions should be made in collaboration with the pastor, and core staff when necessary, to adjust the scope of evaluation and recommendation by limiting focus and/or levels. It is a far better choice to do a good job within feasible limits rather than overextending the council in a way that will lead to poor evaluation and recommendation.

Step III: Collection of Information

1. *Validity, Reliability, Objectivity*—The council and its committees and sub-committees should reverence the necessity for their evaluation to be *valid, reliable* and *objective.* By saying it must be *valid,* we mean two things. First, the information provided by the evaluation must have fidelity or, in a layman's sense, it must be true. Second, the information provided by the evaluation must be generalizable (able to be applied) to similar situations beyond the one in which it was collected. By *reliable* we mean that if the evaluation were repeated it would produce essentially the same findings. If a repetition of the evaluation did not produce essentially similar findings, we should be concerned that the findings were simply random or subjectively biased and therefore meaningless. In stating the necessity to reverence *objectivity,* we are underscoring the need for concern about the "publicness" of the information. If the information and data upon which the evaluation is constructed could only be appreciated and interpreted by particular per-

sons, we would have reason to doubt that not all competent judges would agree on their meaning. Therefore, we could only wonder about the true meaning (objectivity) of the evaluation.

2. *Relevance, Significance, Scope, Credibility*—The council and its committees and sub-committees should appreciate the importance of *relevance, significance, scope* and *credibility*. By *relevance* we mean that the information and data collected and the evaluation based on this information and data should relate to decisions to be made. By *significance* we mean that the information must be weighed for its meaning in relation to the decision. Not all relevant information is equally weighty. By *scope* we mean that the information must relate to all aspects involved in the decision to be made by the pastor, core staff, pastoral staff, particular person-in-charge, etc. If there are six alternatives to be recommended, information that applies to only four lacks scope. By *credibility* we mean that the information can be *trusted* by the decision-makers and those whom pastoral decision-makers and implementers must serve, i.e., those who will be affected by the decisions.

3. *Timeliness, Pervasiveness, Efficiency*—The council, its committees and sub-committees should be concerned with *timeliness, pervasiveness* and *efficiency*. By *timeliness* we mean that the information must come in time to be useful to the decision-maker. The evaluator must guard against the scientific value that argues against publishing findings, until every last element is in. *Late information is worthless information.* It is better in the evaluative situation to have reasonably good information on time than perfect information too late. By *pervasiveness* we mean that the information must get to all the audiences (i.e., to all of the decision-makers) who need it. By *efficiency* we mean that it is possible for an evaluation to mushroom out of all proportion to its value. The imprudent evaluator may produce a mountain of information whose collection imposes an intolerable financial and personnel drain. Proper application of relevance, significance and scope should remedy the grossest inefficiencies. But even when the proposed needed information meets all of these criteria, there are probably still alternative ways for collecting it that differ in terms of the time, costs, personnel, etc. The criterion of efficiency will guide the evaluator to the appropriate alternative.

4. *Decision on Type of Information Needed*—Keeping the principles in mind outlined in 1, 2 and 3 above, the parish council, its committees and sub-committees should decide the type of information that is needed by the pastor, pastoral staff, core staff and persons-in-charge, pertinent to the area being evaluated and the level of the evaluation ("Why?" "What?" or "How?"). Useless information only confuses and inhibits good evaluation and ultimately good decision-making.

5. *Interviewing and Kind of Questions*—The parish council, its committees and sub-committees should decide who needs to be interviewed and what kind of questions need to be asked depending upon the level and focus of evaluation. A preliminary decision should be reached regarding the number of interviews needed and definite arrangements should be decided as to who is interviewed by whom, for how long and when. Of course, such decisions depend ultimately upon cooperation and collaboration between council (researchers and developers) and pastoral decision-makers and implementers. Pastoral decision-makers and implementers will need to be contacted and arrangements made for interviewing. Whenever possible those being interviewed should be alerted ahead of time about the nature of the interview so that they can be better prepared to provide ample and clear information and sometimes supportive documentation.

6. *Decisions on Data-Collection Devices*—The council, its committees and sub-committees should decide ahead of time if the collecting of information will require interviews with persons affected and additional information acquired through surveys, questionnaires, checklists, rating scales and first-hand observations. Such data collection devices are helpful only if they are utilized with a realistic sense of their limitations and with restraint. Such devices can drive everybody "nuts" if they are constantly deployed because someone has a "love affair" with statistics. They should be used only when it's necessary to find out what people think and feel about pertinent issues where there is an important disagreement or ignorance regarding such information. For example, if some people believe that sixty percent of the parishioners are in favor of the parish school and forty percent are not and some people believe the reverse is true, sampling the parish with such a device would settle the disagreement. Such devices should absolutely never be used to deter-

mine with certainty whether it is forty-nine percent or fifty-one percent who believe one way or prefer a particular opinion, etc. Such exactitude doesn't make a damn bit of difference anyway!

7. *Strict Allocation of Time for Collection and Collation of Information*—In addition to making arrangements for interviewing people involved in pastoral decision-making and its implementation, as well as program staff, team ministers and members of organizations, arrangements should also be made for contacting, in person or by mail, people who will contribute information and data for the evaluation through checklists, questionnaires, surveys, observations, etc. Whenever a decision is made to utilize such devices, it is imperative to make arrangements to mail or hand out the instrument, specifying when it should be returned and allowing adequate time to collate the data, for it to be relevant for the evaluation. It is terribly frustrating and unfair to ask people to assist in evaluation by providing relevant information and data received too late to be effectively analyzed and utilized in the evaluation procedure. This error happens too frequently not to mention. Good instruments have been utilized and good data collected only to come in too late to be utilized.

8. *Wide Scope of Data Collection*—The council, its committees and sub-committees should realize that in collecting data they need not confine themselves to pastoral leaders. They need not even confine themselves to parishioners. The scope (level and area of their evaluation) helps to form parameters concerning whom to ask and what to ask, but it does not establish limits. An in-depth evaluation may necessitate going beyond parishioners to the secular community to ask questions or to solicit pertinent information.

9. *What Kinds of Questions to Ask?*—Some of the obvious questions and issues that should be addressed, pertinent to the three different levels of evaluation, are as follows:
(a) *Why?* Why are you doing and being this? What is your purpose? What needs are you addressing? What is the vision of your organization, ministry team or program? Is your vision articulated (written down)? Is the need and purpose for your existence as real and as relevant as it once was? Has anything changed which could or should alter your purpose, vision and aspirations? Was there once a "Why?" for your purpose and now is it forgotten? If so, why? What would renew and revitalize that

sense of purpose? Is there unity and commitment to your purpose among all those involved in your organization, ministry team or program? If not, what are the sources of discord and division? What is the gap between your current experience of what is good and bad about your organization, program or ministry team and its hopes, dreams and aspirations?

(b) *What?* What are the declared strategy, plan of action, goals and objectives that you are trying to reach? What are the actual consequences of your efforts? What is being produced? What are the fruits, the outcomes of your endeavor? What discrepancies, if any, do you see between what you are trying to produce (goals and objectives) and what are, in fact, the real consequences of your effort? What part of your effort is succeeding? What part is failing? Why? How well does what you are trying to produce and/or what you are actually producing measure up to your purpose for being?

(c) *How?* How are decisions made? How are problems identified? How are alternative solutions generated, discussed and decided upon? How are decisions made regarding who is responsible for implementing what? How do you ensure the spiritual foundation for your endeavor? How candidly, honestly and openly do people express their feelings, ideas and values? How is tension handled and the sources of conflict faced up to and resolved? Who communicates what to whom? Who is accountable to whom? Where and how do people receive the leadership, supervision and support to which they are entitled? How do you ensure the opportunity for people with the same or similar responsibility to come together for collegial support, affording them the opportunity to utilize this "collegial experience" to empower and invest in their common leader(s)? What is the emotional and task-orientated climate affecting efficiency within your organization, program or ministry team?

Step IV: Organizing Information That Has Been Collected
1. *Data Organization*—Once the parish council, its committees and sub-committees have conducted interviews and collected information, the data should be organized in a way that allows sub-committees, committees and the parish council as a whole to analyze the information as it applies to the area each is responsible for evaluating, i.e., total parish, divisions, departments, organizations, ministry teams and programs.

2. *Different Dimensions of Data Organization*—The information collected can be organized

around many different dimensions, but at least the council, committees and sub-committees should consider the following:

(a) Organizing the information as it applies to the focus of evaluation, i.e., "Why?" "What?" or "How?"

(b) Organizing the information that documents successes and failures, negative and positive effects pertaining to optional recommendations that must be weighed and considered in preparing recommendations.

(c) Organizing the collected information according to categories such as attitudinal, demographic, survey, interviews, questionnaires, checklists and rating scales.

3. *Organization of Information Summary*—Regardless of how the information is organized, a summary of the information should be developed addressing the questions "Why?" "What?" and "How?" as these pertain to different areas of the parish: total parish, divisions, departments, various organizations, programs and ministry teams. This summary will be utilized by the council as a whole, with its committees and sub-committees in preparation for their review and analysis and as it pertains to their preparation of recommendations. *Organizing the data is not a process of analyzing.* It is a process of discriminating what kind of information applies where, is relevant to what issues and should be at the disposal of which groups. It is a process of cutting down the amount of information to be handled in the analysis which is a part of evaluating and making recommendations concerning the three different levels, "Why?" "What?" and "How?"

Step V: Analyzing the Information

1. *First Step: Prayer*—The first step in analyzing the information should be prayer. The council, its committees and sub-committees would not at all be wasting their time to pray for indifference, i.e., the ability to look at this data and avoid the temptation to bend it, shape it, emphasize or de-emphasize parts to support a preconceived position or to safeguard hurting anybody's feelings, or be unduly critical of anyone or any group that they admittedly just don't like. They should pray for openness and wisdom. They should pray for the ability to openly disagree and effectively embrace any tensions, conflicts or different interpretations among themselves. They should also pray for the ability to speak with candor, courage and conviction. Finally, they should pray to do the best job they can. Realizing for whose benefit their ministry exists, they should pray

for the courage to be indifferent to the consequences of their endeavor, i.e., how much and how it will be utilized.

2. *Collected Information: Basic Evaluative Comments*—The information collected tells the council, its committees and sub-committees something about the questions they were asking regardless of the form, instruments and devices utilized to help pursue this information. The council as a whole, its committees and sub-committees now have the responsibility of looking at the information which is summarized and organized according to area and level and to utilize this information as the foundation for their evaluative comments.

3. *The Judgmental Process*—Whether the council, its committees and sub-committees are analyzing the information (evaluating) or preparing recommendations, the analyzing of information and obtaining evaluative comments are "judgmental" processes. The information and the data are, for the most part, a composite of the judgments of others. The council as a whole, its committees and sub-committees will certainly utilize these judgments, but of course they cannot avoid entering into the judgmental process. In fact, they are the most important principal participants contributing to the judgmental effort called research (evaluation) and development (recommendations).

4. *Some Viable Functions of the Judgmental Process*—In evaluating purpose ("Why?"), objectives and results ("What?") and process ("How?"), the council utilizes the available data organized for the purpose of their analysis, adding their own judgment to point out specific strong and weak points, recommending changes and modifications. In fulfilling these functions, the council will judge whether or not desired objectives and/or results of a program, ministry team, organization, fit well with the espoused purpose or vision of that program, etc. The council will certainly find itself examining the efficiency and adequacy of programs compared to other methods and total needs. Thus, the council will help to set standards of performance and suggest ways of assessing the attainment of these standards. They will help to clarify objectives and, in some cases, may suggest new procedures and new approaches. In looking at the parish as a whole, their evaluation will help to establish priorities among programs, ministry teams and organizations in terms of the best use of limited resources—funds, persons and time. The council can and may suggest

necessary modifications in the total parish vision (pastoral challenge) to fit changing times and circumstances in between the events for total parish discernment as outlined in Chapter 2.

5. *Some Councils Are Big on Evaluations But Short on Recommendations*—In my experience, some councils, for various reasons, prefer to emphasize their evaluative function while de-emphasizing, sometimes to the point of eliminating, the providing of recommendations. Such councils reason that it is not their purpose to develop specific recommendations, but simply to collect, analyze and evaluate. Thus they need only to defend their evaluation in terms of how information was collected, analyzed and judged. When this occurs, however, the council's judgments are frequently and invariably received simply as criticism without any viable and tangible alternatives (recommendations) for improving the situation.

Step VI: Reporting Its Evaluative Findings and Recommendations

1. *Tie Evaluation and Recommendations Together*—The basic function of a council serving in a research (evaluation) and development (recommendation) capacity is to present a written report elaborated by a verbal report to the pastor, core staff and other pastoral decision-makers and implementers, weaving together its evaluation and recommendation. Sometimes the written and verbal reports are given to the entire parish at an open meeting. As recommenders, their basic function is to develop proposals for alternative courses of action to be presented to those with the authority and responsibility for choosing from among these alternatives or rejecting them. Typically, one recommendation will not be enough. The council should, in light of its evaluation, offer alternative recommendations and rank order its preferred course of action from among the alternatives in accordance with its evaluative comments. Needless to say, a mere recommendation, stated as such, untied to the evaluation, will not be enough. When deciders turn down proposals or delay implementing a proposal, it is not usually because they disagree with the recommendation. More often it is simply because the recommenders have not adequately "done their evaluative homework."

2. *The Written Statement of Evaluations and Recommendations*—The written statement containing evaluative comments and recommendations should be brief and concise. It should contain background information identifying the level(s) and focus or foci of the evaluation and recommendations being addressed. The report should explain the process used to collect and analyze information to make judgments and to develop alternative recommendations. The pastoral decision-makers and implementers need to know that the council has gone through the proper and appropriate channels and that the people who will be affected by the proposal or who have experiences pertaining to the evaluative aspects have participated, at least indirectly, in this process of evaluation and recommendations. When the council has a preference for a particular recommendation, it should indicate why it thinks other alternatives are less desirable and why it rejected other possible alternatives. This will indicate to the pastoral decision makers and implementers the scope of the investigation undertaken by the parish council and hopefully will show that all possibilities were considered.

3. *Levels on Consenus*—In elaborating on their evaluation and recommendation(s), it will be of great help to the pastoral decision-makers and implementers, as well as to the council itself, to articulate their level of consensus regarding various evaluative judgments and recommendations. As evaluators, was there total unanimity in their agreement regarding the strengths and weaknesses, etc.? Were their recommendations reached unanimously, consensually or by a split vote? Sharing their internal struggle at achieving good evaluative judgments and arriving at good recommendations can be as illuminating and sometimes more enlightening than the distilled fruits of this effort.

4. *Keeping the Focus and Level Clear*—Above all else, in reporting its evaluation and recommendations the council should be clear and systematic in addressing the three levels of evaluation (and recommendation) and the area addressed, i.e., the parish as a whole, a particular division, department, ministry team, program or organization. Nothing is more disconcerting than a written or verbal report containing evaluative comments and recommendations that is unclear as to when it is addressing the whole parish or a particular component of the parish. This is particularly important to remember in proposing alternatives and making recommendations. Does the recommendation address purpose, objectives, process or the alignment of these three levels of evaluation? Does the recommendation pertain to the total parish, to a particular organization or ministry team, etc.?

5. *How Will the Council Know When It Has Accomplished Its Ministry?*—Developing recommendations is not an easy task. It is a job that calls for solid research and careful analysis. What is perhaps more significant is that this is essentially a new role for lay people in our parishes. It calls for a new set of skills, a new determination to measure the value of what we are being and doing for one another and for those beyond ourselves and a new kind of relationship among us as clergy, religious and lay people sharing an apostolate. But there can be no doubt that a parish council which has learned the skills of evaluating and recommending is a viable and powerful force for the well-being of the apostolic organization we call parish.

If a council adopts this function, accepting this ministry, the result will be far better communication and sharing of information among the staff and among various divisions, departments, organizations, programs, and ministry teams, etc. Pastoral decision-makers and implementers and the parish as a whole will develop a critical attitude regarding the importance of effective decision-making and direction-setting. The information provided through such a ministry provides the basis for healthy accountability and the increased capability of everyone in the parish to identify with its collective effort. The net result will be increased support for successful ministry and decreased demand for unnecessary and unsuccessful efforts. At the same time, research and development by the parish council is a tremendous opportunity for building the morale and providing affirmation for all those involved in pastoral decision-making and its implementation. The most basic test to help the council to determine if it is doing what it is supposed to be doing in this ministry will be the effective response of the pastoral decision-makers and implementers to the council as they adopt this ministry. Done properly and responsibly, this ministry is experienced as very supportive, fulfilling a great and urgent need and as providing the needed resources for collective and individual growth.